The RUBBER BAND

ENDORSEMENTS

Christy has a natural style, writing about serious subject matter, but manages to lace it with humor. It's very clear that she knows kids. Each character faces challenges reflecting real life issues for children today—from health problems to broken families. There's a sense of expectation throughout. These kids will rise to be overcomers.

I look forward to the next installment in *The Rubber Band* series.

—**Francine Rivers**, New York Times bestselling author

The RUBBER BAND

Dream big Dreams and Trust God to help you achieve them!

— Christy Hoss

CHRISTY HOSS

Is. 41:9-10   Romans 8:28

I can do all things through Christ who gives me strength! Philippians 4:13

Copyright Notice

The Rubber Band

First edition. Copyright © 2020 by Christy Hoss. The information contained in this book is the intellectual property of Christy Hoss and is governed by United States and International copyright laws. All rights reserved. No part of this publication, either text or image, may be used for any purpose other than personal use. Therefore, reproduction, modification, storage in a retrieval system, or retransmission, in any form or by any means, electronic, mechanical, or otherwise, for reasons other than personal use, except for brief quotations for reviews or articles and promotions, is strictly prohibited without prior written permission by the publisher.

This is a work of fiction. Names, characters, businesses, places, events, locales, and incidents are either the products of the author's imagination or used in a fictitious manner. Any resemblance to actual persons, living or dead, or actual events is purely coincidental.

Cover and Interior Design: Derinda Babcock

Editor(s): Kim Autrey, Linda Rondeau, Deb Haggerty

Author Represented By: Cyle Young Literary Elite Agency

PUBLISHED BY: Elk Lake Publishing, Inc., 35 Dogwood Drive, Plymouth, MA 02360, 2020

Library Cataloging Data

Names: Hoss, Christy (Christy Hoss)

The Rubber Band / Christy Hoss

190 p. 23cm × 15cm (9in × 6 in.)

Identifiers: ISBN-13: 978-1-951970-62-8 (paperback) | 978-1-951970-63-5 (trade paperback) | 978-1-951970-64-2 (e-book)

Key Words: Middle-grade, bullying, band, discipline,

LCCN: 2020942890 Fiction

DEDICATION

To the Cannard twins—
I continue to be inspired by your successes

To Kenwood Elementary School—
Thank you for years of inspiration

ACKNOWLEDGMENTS

Kevin Lee Hoss, my beyond-wonderful husband, you are my daily inspiration. Thank you for believing in me and walking with me every step of this journey. I look forward to many more years, enjoying our dreams together.

To my most favorite sister in the whole, wide world, Cindy Stromlund Thomas, for inspiring my writing journey with a "Nothing" book when we were kids.

Thank you to my Daddy, David Stromlund, for your generosity.

To my writing group gals: Erin Briggs, Kitty Briggs, Claudia Millerick, Francine Rivers, Jackie Tisthammer, and Lynette Winters—thank you for encouraging and inspiring me from chapter one to the end. Here's to many more in The Rubber Band series.

Thank you to my sisters in Christ at Elk Lake Publishing, Inc.—Susan Stewart for believing in *The Rubber Band* before it was written, and Deb Haggerty for wanting the finished product. Your patience and prayers with me to find a literary agent always gave me hope. Thank you, Kim Autrey and Derinda Babcock for your patience with me through the editing process.

Thank you to Sarah Gorman of Cyle Young Literary Elite Agency for referring me to my agent Chrysa Keenon. Sarah, I hope your film-making dreams come true.

The RUBBER BAND

Thank you Chrysa Keenon and Cyle Young for signing me. I love being a part of the C.Y.L.E. Agency family and its resourceful support for its clients.

Thank you, Laura Christenson of Blogging Bistro for your marketing expertise.

I thank God, my Father, for His faithfulness along this journey.

For from Him, and through Him, and in Him are all things.
To Him be the glory forever! Amen (Romans 11:6 NIV).

CHAPTER ONE

TROUBLEMAKER

"What's it going to be, Pinhead?" Bossy Becca sits back, folding her arms.

I squeeze my fists so tight my fingers go numb. But I do feel something. Clenched inside my right fist is the rubber band from the card game we are playing. Behind my back, I secretly stretch the band as far as I can around my thumb and pointer finger. She is going to regret challenging me.

Just like slow motion in a movie, my arm comes from behind my back with ammunition locked and loaded.

SNAP!

The rubber band flies from my finger-gun directly at Bossy Becca. Her eyes cross as the rubber band springs toward her nose. Fortunately, I have terrible aim. The elastic ring sails past her left ear and onto the carpet behind her.

Fortunately for me, I miss—averting a certain disaster that would come from using a rubber band the wrong way in the classroom.

Bossy Becca's mouth curves into a devilish smirk then turns downward into a pouty frown. She rubs her left eye until it turns the color of a red crayon. The fire in her eyes changes to raging waterfalls running down her cheeks. She puts a hand over her eye and scrunches up her face, "Miss Crenshaw!"

The RUBBER BAND

Her voice sends me into the time zone where only I can move, and everything around me freezes. Even the hands on the atomic clock stop. In a split second, I am set up, betrayed.

Miss Crenshaw rushes to Becca and wraps her arms around the sniffling girl. I know Bossy Becca is faking, but her acting abilities from drama club convince Miss Crenshaw she is injured. After all, Becca is full-on sobbing now, and Miss Crenshaw's look tells me things aren't going to end in just an apology.

"Edison Taylor." Oh no! She used my first and last name, like when I get in trouble at home, only Mom uses my first, middle, and last name.

"Go see Principal Haymaker immediately."

What's going on? Am I watching one of those corny kid's TV comedies, or is this one of my made-up daydreams?

No such luck.

I don't believe this is happening to me. Edison Taylor. I've been going to Wildwood Elementary School since kindergarten, and, for the first time in my elementary school career, I'm sitting outside the principal's office, in trouble. I'm not a troublemaker.

In fact, according to Miss Crenshaw's comments on my last third-grade report card, I'm a peacekeeper, always trying to solve other people's problems.

The school secretary, Mrs. Rogers, is peering at me over the top of her pointy-rimmed glasses. Her glasses make her look like an angry cat. Her look says I'm guilty just because I'm sitting on what we call the hot seat next to Principal Haymaker's door with the frosty window and black capital letters announcing he's in charge. I really don't want him to open the door and find me, the peacekeeper, in trouble.

CHRISTY HOSS

The whole school knows I would never do what Bossy Becca says I did, except for Mrs. Rogers who is watching my every move in between answering the phone and working on her computer. Every time I look up, I find her giving me the squinty-eye look and shaking her head.

How long have I been sitting here? Minutes, hours, days? I just want to get this over with. What could possibly be taking Mr. Haymaker so long?

This school day started like all the other days and not, not even fifteen minutes into a routine day, I'm up next to see Mr. Haymaker, the principal.

I quietly count off seconds in sync with the wall clock when Mrs. Rogers leaves her desk to put up a brightly colored poster of musical instruments and people singing on the announcement board. In bold letters, the poster reads:

Sun Valley Talent Show Contest

Auditions now being scheduled–Apply online

Oliver and I should give the contest a try. With his keyboard and my guitar talents, we might become the next Simon and Garfunkel. My best friend, Emmanuel, is getting better at playing the bass, so maybe I'll look up the contest when I get home. For now, I have unexpected things to deal with, like not knowing what will happen once I am behind Principal Haymaker's door.

I notice my left sneaker is untied. I can't be in trouble and face the principal with my shoe untied, so I reach down to fix it. The chair cushion next to me squeezes out air as some larger person occupies it.

Finishing the loop tie on my shoe, I turn my head, peeking through my shaggy bangs to see who is sitting next to me. The checkered shoes and ripped jeans look familiar.

Swallowing what feels like a rock, I realize the person sitting next to me is none other than Rocky "Roadkill" Espinosa. No one wants to mess with the fourth grader who

The Rubber Band

is never without his drumsticks, beating on everything in sight.

We secretly call him Roadkill because if you cross him wrong, he will run you over flat like a skunk under the tires of a semitruck. He spends a lot of time waiting to see Principal Haymaker. Rumor is he lives in a court-ordered group home for delinquent boys. His well-worn black leather jacket is unzipped, revealing a white T-shirt declaring "Bite Me" in bold fluorescent lettering.

Principal Haymaker's door opens before I dare look Roadkill in the face. The PE teacher, Mr. Bleeker, comes out, takes one look at me, and declares, "I never thought I'd see the two of you together in the principal's office." He chuckles, heads to Mrs. Roger's desk, and says, "Let's go ahead with those equipment requisitions, Doris—I mean Mrs. Rogers."

I hear Mrs. Rogers giggle, but only one thing is on my mind—my turn to go behind the closed door of the principal's office.

"Edison Taylor, you may come in." Principal Haymaker summons.

Standing up without a look toward Roadkill, I obey the commanding voice.

"Close the door please and have a seat." Principal Haymaker motions for the chair, and I wiggle into it until my back is tight against the wooden slats. Sweat drizzles down my back, sealing my T-shirt to the varnish. I swallow hard, grip the chair's arms, and stare at the floor. On the plastic mat under his desk, I locate two paper clips, one pushpin, and a rubber band like the one that got me into trouble.

"Mr. Taylor, I understand we had a bit of trouble this morning. I must say, I am quite disappointed to see you in the office under these circumstances."

I locate another stray pushpin near the trash can.

"I'm happy to hear Miss Chang was not mortally injured by your infraction. The ice pack Miss Crenshaw immediately applied should reduce any swelling and deter a black eye from developing."

Swelling? Black eye? Who is Bossy Becca kidding?

"In the meantime, I will have to notify your parents. You'll have to write an apology letter to Miss Crenshaw and to Becca as well."

Oh, no. I can't let a lie get that far.

Mr. Haymaker leans forward, resting his elbows on the desk. His hands come together like a church steeple. "Did you or did you not shoot a rubber band at Rebecca Chang while playing math games in Miss Crenshaw's classroom this morning?"

I didn't hurt Becca. In fact, the rubber band missed her because I have terrible aim. But I did shoot it with the intention of hitting her, just not in the eye. Now, she is the one stretching the truth to make me look bad.

This is what really happened. It replays like a movie in my brain.

Bossy Becca sat down in front of me with one of her fire-breathing, dragon stares, shooting flames at me. "Deal, Eddie." I didn't want her as my math games partner. There is a reason the entire school secretly calls her Bossy Becca.

"I'm not happy about this arrangement either, but class rules say the order of finishing math warm-up is how you get a game partner. I need to follow the rules to get my star for the day. I don't want to break my perfect record."

The RUBBER BAND

I ignored her comment. Everyone gets a star for good behavior, every day. The only way you don't get a star is if you get in trouble.

Beginning the game, I tried to match the number on the overturned card using all the math functions we had learned with the five laid out cards.

"Eight plus seven is fifteen. Fifteen minus two is thirteen, thirteen plus ten is twenty-three, and twenty-three plus zero is …" I pounded my palms on my legs for a drum roll. "… twenty-three!" I scooped up the cards in victory, raised my arms to the imaginary rejoicing crowd in the stadium seats shouting, Eddie! Eddie! Eddie!

Miss Crenshaw looked concerned and put her finger to her mouth, shushing me.

"Knock it off, Pinhead. It's only one turn. I'll burn you this time." Becca fingered the end of one of her long, black braids. I replaced the five cards I'd won, and Becca turned the next number to find, thirteen.

She leaned forward from her crisscross applesauce position, loomed over the row of cards, picked up a couple, mumbled, and put them back. She repeated this action several times, sat back, and kicked her legs out in front of her creating an angle with her sockless, shoed feet.

"This is impossible. The numbers you put out are too high to do anything with, and most of them are even. There's no way I can put any of these cards together to make thirteen." The fire returned to her eyes.

"Do you give up?" I was ready to win this round and douse the fire in her eyes before she could add a snarky comment to fuel the flame.

"To get the number thirteen, add twelve plus ten, subtract seven, subtract two, and add zero." I scooped the five cards up ready to receive the imaginary stadium crowd's victory chants again, but instead, get the red-hot face of Bossy Becca pushing her nose to my nose. Her breath smelled like a bacon burp.

She jabbed her finger, poking me in the chest. "You cheated! I'm telling Miss Crenshaw."

That's when it happened.

SNAP!

"Mr. Taylor. I'm waiting for your answer." Principal Haymaker's stern voice ends the movie replay in my brain. He uses the tone of voice I've only heard when he talks to kids in trouble.

Cradling my head in my hands, I stare at the floor. This day just can't get any worse.

CHAPTER TWO

PRINCIPAL HAYMAKER

Principal Haymaker's office is silent, and if another pushpin drops to the floor, I'll hear it. I wish for a hot air balloon to float me away from Wildwood Elementary School, but it won't help me escape fast enough. I need something much faster, like a rocket.

With no rescue rocket in sight, I breathe a deep breath, puff it out, slouch my shoulders, and hope for the best.

"Yes. I did."

Principal Haymaker raises an eyebrow, making his forehead look lopsided.

"I realize this is unusual behavior for you, and I've never had to bring you to the office in trouble, but I have to treat the problem like I would do for any other student. But since it's your first and only offense, ever, I am not going to suspend you."

Relief. I pull my shoulders back to better posture and scoot the chair closer to the desk.

"I have something better, more productive in mind. This coming weekend is campus clean-up day, and there are many projects to be done. You will report here to me by nine a.m. on Saturday to be assigned your job. Will there be any conflicts with that, Mr. Taylor?" Principal Haymaker leans on his desk and peers at me over his reading glasses. His steely blues eyes

The RUBBER BAND

remind me of Superman and his X-ray vision looking right through my skin and bones to my racing heart.

Swallowing hard, I squeak out an answer. "No, sir."

"Good. I'll make the arrangements with your parents."

I remain in the chair, glued to the back again. Principal Haymaker writes on his notepad and without looking up says, "You're excused, Mr. Taylor."

I wiggle the grasp of my sweaty shirt from the chair and head out the door. Roadkill eyeballs me with a silly grin on his face. "See yah later, Pinhead."

Mrs. Rogers gives him a stern rebuke, and I make my way back to third grade. Math lesson is half over, and Miss Crenshaw walks around the room helping students. She smiles, but everyone else's eyes are on me as I sit in my desk.

My best friend, Emmanuel leans over and whispers, "How'd it go?"

"I don't want to talk about it. Maybe at recess." I notice Bossy Becca has a reusable ice pack sitting on her desk as she scribbles away at the math problem sheet.

There is nothing to do about my situation, and my enthusiasm for math problems is dead. I can't let this get the best of me. I am a peacekeeper and will face this like I've just resolved World War Three. I pick up my pencil and get down to solving math problems.

Despite distraction from my wandering mind, I manage to turn in a finished math paper by the time the recess bell rings. I join Emmanuel on the basketball court shooting hoops with my twin brother, Oliver. We aren't identical, but in some ways, we are very much alike. Take for example, how we feel about Bossy Becca.

"Hey, Eddie. What did you do to Bossy Becca to make Miss Crenshaw send you to Mr. Haymaker's office?" Emmanuel passes the ball to me, and I put the ball through the hoop with a quick lay-up.

"I shot a rubber band at Bossy Becca."

Emmanuel and Oliver freeze, missing the rebounding basketball bouncing away.

"Whoah! That's why she had the ice pack? You hit her straight on in the eye? Way to go, bro!" Oliver holds his fist out for me to give it a victory bump.

"I missed!" I throw my hands up into the air.

"What?" Emmanuel and Oliver exclaim in unison.

"The rubber band flew past her head."

"Oh." The guys shake their heads. They know Bossy Becca is a drama queen with a mean streak. She loves to tattle and get other kids in trouble.

"Bro, you don't need to say anything else." Emmanuel puts his hand on my shoulder.

"Yeah, but we're going to have to work on your aim." Oliver's fist punches me in the side of my arm.

"I really wanted to hit her. She was giving me the attitude, and I couldn't take it anymore."

"She's a big, fat liar! If you didn't hit her with the rubber band, why are you in trouble? Didn't you tell Principal Haymaker what really happened?" Emmanuel always has my back.

"Yeah, Eddie. Principal Haymaker knows you'd never do anything like that to anyone—not even Bossy Becca." Oliver fetches the basketball and shoots from the free throw line.

"I wanted to tell him, but … he asked me if I shot the rubber band. I couldn't lie and say I didn't because I DID shoot the rubber band. It just missed Bossy Becca's face by a hundred yards."

Emmanuel grabs the rebound and holds the ball. "You have to explain the whole story to him. It's not right. She needs to get in trouble too."

"If I could do it all over again, I would take better aim and hit her right between the eyes." I pretend like I'm aiming

The RUBBER BAND

for her face. "Pewpew!" I shoot an imaginary rubber band into the sky. "I won't miss this time."

Emmanuel and Oliver look up like they are watching the imaginary rubber band hit Bossy Becca's nose.

"If you ever decide to do it again, make sure you let us know, so we can watch." Oliver steals the ball from Emmanuel and shoots a lay-up.

"If there is a next time." I get the rebound. "After I answered yes, he didn't give me a chance to explain, so now I have to come here Saturday and work with the cleanup crew to do community service."

I pass Emmanuel the ball, and he takes a shot from the free throw line. "That's not too bad. I thought you might get detention or worse yet, be suspended."

"Principal Haymaker said since it was my first offense, ever, if I come and work the campus cleanup day, it won't go on my permanent record."

"So, I guess we aren't going to the movies like we planned?" Emmanuel fetches the ball and passes it to Oliver.

"Did he call Mom and Dad?" Oliver hangs on to the ball, stopping the game.

"Of course, he did!" My voice booms. "It's his job to call the parents when a kid gets in trouble."

"Oh bro. I'm so sorry. Mom and Dad won't like this. You're going to lose your allowance for a month!" Oliver shoots but misses his attempt at a three-pointer. "They can give the money to me instead!"

The ball bounces, rolls into the grass, and rests at the feet of Roadkill. Frozen in fear for what might happen next, we eyeball each other. I'll be road-pizza for sure. Roadkill always walks the playground alone, and his actions can be unpredictable. At any given moment, he might clobber you if you look at him wrong. I've never once seen him smile.

Roadkill picks up the ball and walks toward us. Our sneakers glue to the asphalt court, unable to move. I swallow what feels like a boulder in my throat. Every step he takes brings doom closer, and I wonder how we will die or if Roadkill will show us mercy. I close my eyes as his hot breath puffs against my face. The basketball presses between our bellies.

"You lost this, Pinhead."

The rumor is Roadkill has controlling powers like a hypnotist. I don't dare look into his eyes for fear he'll force me to do something I'll regret. Instead, I stare at the ball pressed between us.

Roadkill backs up. The ball drops and bounces behind me. I open my eyes long enough to notice Roadkill is wearing a different T-shirt. This one sports the school mascot snarling over the words, "Wildwood Elementary School."

As Roadkill walks away, he looks over his shoulder and says, "See you Saturday, Pinhead."

Chapter Three

Community Service

Instead of sleeping late and eating my favorite fruit-flavored cereal directly out of the box, I sit in the back seat of the family van on the way to school to serve my sentence for the rubber band incident. If I could, I would gladly just go back in time to stop my fingers from springing the rubber band. But this isn't a comic book story where time travel is always a possibility. I have to face reality.

My reality was facing my parents after they heard the story from Principal Haymaker. I had to repeat my version of the story at dinner. Mom was nearly in tears and didn't say much. Dad kept shaking his head saying he thought I didn't have a mean bone in my body. Oliver kept giving me our secret look that meant we would talk later. I lost my allowance for a month and will be doing extra chores not on my usual list.

But the ultimate punishment is happening today, spending my free time at the school playground, working like a county prisoner cleaning the side of the freeway in orange jumpsuits, wearing ankle chains.

I recognize most of the kid-faces when we pull into the school parking lot. This could be fun after all. I hop out of the van and wave goodbye to Oliver and my parents. They have too many errands to run to spend the day working at the school with me.

The RUBBER BAND

Principal Haymaker stands in the middle of a group of adults, holding a shovel. He looks like a normal person wearing jeans and a T-shirt instead of his usual dress shirt and tie as he gives instructions and hands out jobs to the volunteers.

"Welcome, Mr. Taylor. I've got just the job for you." Principal Haymaker wastes no time in handing me a pair of gloves and a large trash bag. "You'll be walking the perimeter of the grounds picking up trash, especially the stuff that gets caught in the bushes and against the fence." He hands me a small rake and pick. "Start at the baseball field and work your way around to the playground. Your partner is already out there waiting for you."

Oh, good. At least I won't be walking the perimeter, alone.

"Break time is 10:30, and I'll blow a whistle for refreshments in the multipurpose room. Now, off you go. I expect the bag to be overflowing by the time you are done."

"Yes, sir." I slip the gloves on, grab the trash bag and tools, and run to the ballfield like hungry cheetahs were chasing me. Bright sunshine blocks the view of my partner waiting on the dugout bench. As he stands, there is no denying a pair of drumsticks sticking out of his back jeans' pocket.

I'd rather be walking the perimeter alone.

"Pinhead!" Roadkill walks up and pokes his Band-Aid wrapped finger at my chest. "My job just got easier. I'll supervise while you do my share of cleanup."

Frozen like an ice sculpture in a fancy buffet line, I can barely breathe. Not only am I mostly innocent of the crime, but I am being punished in the worst way ever. I may not live to shoot another rubber band.

If I don't produce a bag full of trash for Principal Haymaker, my spotless name will be blackened forever. Now, I'll have to work twice as hard to fill Roadkill's bag as well.

Roadkill leans against the wooden fence like a construction supervisor watching my every move while I pick up every piece of trash down to the miniscule gum wrapper. I don't dare look up at his face. This will be the cleanest fence line ever.

Sweat drips to the end of my nose, and I pause to wipe it off on my shoulder. I take the opportunity to sneak a peek. Roadkill is sitting in the shade under the maple tree, and I can see the wires of his earbuds. His eyes closed, he seems wrapped up in a tune, tapping out a beat with his drumsticks. He spins the sticks between his fingers, tapping his foot like hitting a base drum, then resumes beating at imaginary drums and cymbals.

I shake my head. This job would go a lot faster if I'd brought music too, especially since I am doing double duty filling two bags instead of one. I take turns between the two bags with each piece of trash I find. At the rate I am going, I'll be here until dinner. Just thinking about food makes my stomach grumble.

I'm a safe distance from Roadkill to peek and see if he is still pounding out a beat. I stop, pull my T-shirt up to wipe my brow, and look in his direction. The shady spot beneath the tree is vacant.

"Pinhead, my bag is only half full." Roadkill's voice turns me into an ice sculpture again, but the morning's heat is melting me.

There is no way I will be able to fill two bags. I want to stuff him inside his trash bag and drag him back to Principal Haymaker. But, before I can say a word, the whistle blows for break time. Roadkill grabs both bags, dumps one's contents into another, and hands me an empty bag. He struts off to the multipurpose room leaving me empty handed.

There is no doubt in my mind I'll be here all day.

The RUBBER BAND

Roadkill is handing Principal Haymaker his bag full of my trash when I arrive dragging my empty offering.

"Wow, Rocky, you worked hard this morning. Keep this up, and you'll be going home after our second shift. Great job." Principal Haymaker pats him on the back and reaches to take my bag. A few remnants of trash stick to its sides, so it looks like I have done a little something. "Edison. I thought you were more ambitious than this."

One look at Roadkill and all thoughts of turning him in right then and there leave my mind instantly. He could stare down a hungry lion from a fresh steak dinner.

I shove my hands in my pockets and stare at Principal Haymaker's perfectly tied tennis shoes. I don't know what to say except, "I'm sorry. I'll try harder after break." It must have been a good answer because he allows me to pass into the coolness of the airconditioned multipurpose room for snacks.

After a bag of chips and an apple juice box, I pick up my bag and walk out to the fence. I want to get a head start since I'll be working for two people. I didn't have the courage to turn on Roadkill because I value my life. Besides, Bossy Becca will always be there to make me miserable, and I don't need another problem.

As I focus on the ground before me, a shadow looms into my view. The shadow has drumsticks like antennae on a praying mantis. Hopes of filling my bag and leaving early crumble like a dry cookie. Roadkill has returned.

I muster enough courage to speak. "I suppose you need another bag filled for you, and I have to do it or else." I look him square in the eye ready to face my sentence. He says nothing but takes my bag and rake and goes to work bagging trash twice as fast as I had been moving.

This time I'm not an ice sculpture, but I am still frozen in my shoes. I can't believe what I see. Scraping garbage out of the bushes and shoveling it into my bag, Roadkill works with great fury to fill both our bags. I can't let him do all the work alone.

I hold the bag open as he tosses in the trash. Neither of us say a word as we work our way around the edge of the school fence line. We finish the job just in time for lunch.

Principal Haymaker blows the whistle again, and all the workers head back to the reward of a pizza lunch. I'm still in shock at Roadkill's actions as I hand in my overflowing bag.

"Now this is more like what I'd expect from you, Mr. Taylor. Excellent work."

I smile and glance toward Roadkill who is already at a table, wolfing down his share of pizza.

I want to give Roadkill the credit, but there is a slice or two of pepperoni calling my name. Piling my plate up with the cheesy goodness and grabbing a bottle of water, I search the room for him, but he's already left. He couldn't have gotten far. I take my lunch outside and search the playground. I find him sitting under the maple tree, drumming rhythm to music only he can hear.

Roadkill seems oblivious to the world around him, and a crazy thought crosses my mind.

CHAPTER FOUR

Daring Idea

I'd been thinking it over since getting home from the campus cleanup. If I can muster the courage, my plan will be put into action at lunch recess. But lunch is three hours away. In the meantime, I have to deal with Bossy Becca.

Becca finishes her math warm-ups before me, and truthfully, I'm stalling because I really don't want to be stuck playing math games with her again. Unfortunately, Miss Crenshaw notices everything.

"Eddie, would you please start a math game. Rebecca is in need of a partner."

Busted.

I don't have a choice. All eyeballs are on me as I shove my pencil in my desk, grab my paper, and drop my work in the finished work box. You would think I'd stuffed Oliver's rock collection in my pockets as I move slowly. I feel like I'm wearing one hundred-pound shoes as I drag my feet toward a sneering Becca. She's already dealing the cards for the game and is rolling the rubber band between her palms like she's making a clay snake. Just like a snake, she slithers into my face as soon as I sit crisscross applesauce facing her.

"Did you have fun at community service day?" She couldn't wait to rub the humiliation in my face.

I scoop up three cards adding to seventeen and take my turn silently.

The RUBBER BAND

"I heard you got stuck working with Roadkill. I'm surprised you're still alive and breathing."

"It's your turn, Becca." I turn the cards over. She has to make fourteen.

"Guess what, Pinhead? I've been chosen to sing the National Anthem at Granite Hill High School's homecoming." She runs her fingers over the cards trying to get to fourteen. "I was picked over fifteen other people."

She still hasn't gotten fourteen, but she seems to think talking about herself is more important.

"Homecoming is a humongous deal when you get to high school. There's a king and queen and a formal dance. It's way more fun than the sock hops we have in the multipurpose room."

My elbows bend, and I slouch backward on the carpet. "Are you going to play your hand, or should I?" My patience tank is running low, with no filling station in sight. My mom always says patience is something I need more of, but I don't feel like getting more on Bossy Becca's terms.

She picks up two cards, not caring she can possibly have two more, as she babbles on about things I can care less about. I don't mind because as I turn over the next few cards, I get to pick up all five. Normally, Bossy Becca would pitch a fit, but she takes her turn, and once again misses picking up extra cards.

"I'm going to be homecoming queen one day. I've been practicing the parade wave like the Queen of England does to the crowds." The back of her hand faces me as she waves. She points her chin and nose upward with a snooty, sour grin.

"You look like you ate a lemon." I can't resist that one.

"You'll be eating lemons the day I am crowned."

I'd like to crown her right now with a knuckle sandwich, but memories of the rubber band incident from last week stop me. Besides, I'm not a violent person and would never carry out my secret thoughts of punching her in her bragging mouth. I don't want another trip to see Principal Haymaker. Instead, I turn over more cards and find myself unable to get the number.

Becca taps her fingers on the floor as I contemplate my move. Her breath smells like green peppers and onions, and I decide to secretly call her "omelet breath."

Before I can solve the number nineteen, Miss Crenshaw rings the attention bell to clean up for announcements and the Pledge of Allegiance. "We have a special treat to start our day. Becca, would you please come forward."

Omelet breath makes her way to the front.

"Becca has been chosen to sing our national anthem at a special event, and I thought it would be good for her to practice for us as our flag salute this morning. Let's stand and face the flag with our hands over our hearts."

Did Bossy Becca really need this attention to make her head any bigger? As we place our hands on our hearts, I notice a change in Bossy Becca. She gazes at the flag with perfect posture, takes a deep breath, and belts out the words we hear all the time before sporting events.

"Oh, say can you see, by the dawn's early light." Her face beams with patriotic pride. I've heard our national anthem sung terribly on TV because some of the notes are hard to reach, and some singers shouldn't have been trying to reach them, but when Bossy Becca comes to the hard notes, my heart skips. Her pitch-perfect voice flows as naturally as her matching actions. I can't decide if she is overly dramatic or super patriotic.

"The land of the free, and the home of the brave." Bossy Becca's animated hands rise in praise and point to the flag as the class erupts in applause, and Miss Crenshaw wipes her eyes with a tissue.

The RUBBER BAND

Bossy Becca's face shines like the neon lights of the Ferris wheel at night. I forget about her being a drama queen. Instead, I feel like hugging her. Me, Edison Taylor, hugging Bossy Becca? Yep, that's what I thought too. Impossible, not going to happen.

"Thank you, Rebecca. That was simply wonderful." Miss Crenshaw takes care of the hugging for me. "You will certainly wow the crowd at the homecoming game, don't you agree, class?" Everyone agrees in unison, except for me. I remain speechless.

Miss Crenshaw gets us working on our math lesson, but for the first time, math doesn't interest me. All I can think of is Bossy Becca would get the golden buzzer if she was on one of those talent shows.

I always sit with my brother and Emmanuel at lunch recess, but today I have a plan. I've been thinking about my plan since Saturday. My heart rate rockets as I approach the empty picnic table. No one usually sits at the table because it is under the big oak tree, and most of the time, has fresh bird poop the custodian hadn't cleaned up yet. I locate Roadkill sitting on the end of the bench with his back toward me. I take a deep breath and swallow hard. My lunch box hits the table as I plop my bottom on the bench across from Roadkill.

His eyes meet mine as I unzip my bag. My voice squeaks, "How ya doing, Road, um, Rocky?" His silent chewing tells me to mind my own business. I pull out my PBJ, hoping I won't die.

"You dropped your lunch box in bird poop."

In my gallant attempt to be friendly, I'd made a total fool of myself. Before I can gather my stuff, give up on my quest, and move to another table, Roadkill bursts into belly-busting laughter.

I don't believe my ears. Roadkill can laugh. He's laughing so loud, the table next to us stops talking. He convulses and snorts, grabbing his stomach like he might hurl the lunch he swallowed. When the next-door table begins to laugh too, I slip out a nervous giggle and join the fun.

Amazing what fresh bird droppings can do to ease my nerves.

While everyone gets back to eating, I remember my quest.

"Thanks for what you did on Saturday." I take an extra big bite of my sandwich to fill my whole mouth for fear I might say something stupid and get pulverized. Silence from the other side of the table makes me want to move, but if there is such a thing as instinct, it kicks in, and I stay put, shoveling my food in as fast as I can, hoping to be dismissed by yard duty as soon as possible.

I imagine hearing the basketball court calling my name, and I want to be alive to play hoops with Emmanuel and Oliver. Where are my best buds in my time of need? I put myself in harm's way by sitting with Roadkill, and they abandon me.

Roadkill guzzles his half pint of milk, belches, and wipes his face on his sleeve. As he reaches behind his back, I prepare to duck and cover like he had a weapon. I think I've seen too many police shows because he pulls drumsticks from his back pocket and starts thumping a rhythm.

Once I breathe again, I finish what I'd started.

"Road, um, Rocky. I just want to let you know how much I appreciate you filling my trash bags on Saturday." His face wrinkles like a raisin, and I know he took my gratefulness in the wrong way. "I mean, you personally weren't in the trash bags, you put trash in them, but they weren't full of you." I stop talking and gulp a mouthful from my water bottle. "Can

The RUBBER BAND

I just say thank you? You made me look good to Principal Haymaker."

Roadkill stops tapping his drumsticks, holds up his palm, clearly saying, "stop blabbering, you sound like a fool."

"Forget it, Eddie. Consider us even."

Wait? He didn't call me his favorite nickname.

"Even?" My eyes grow so big it feels like they won't fit in my sockets and will pop out into the bird poop on the table.

"Yeah. You didn't turn me in for not working the first part of the morning. No one has covered for me before. We're even."

I want to pinch myself, but I don't. Instead, I muster up the courage to follow through on my crazy idea.

"Have you ever thought of playing drums in a band?"

The drumsticks stop tapping along with my heart. "I'm not a band nerd, and I never will be."

I've never thought of Roadkill being a nerd. He is more like a motorcycle gang leader.

"Not that kind of band. I mean like a garage band—for fun. My brother plays the keyboard, and I play guitar. We need a drummer. I figure since you are never without your sticks, maybe you need someplace to use them besides someone's head." OOPS! Did I have to say that?

I now understand the saying "so thick you could cut it with a knife" because Roadkill's silence feels like a cheese wedge from the deli. I should've kept my crazy idea to myself, forever. Something inside me keeps pushing the idea forward.

"Oliver and I play after school and on the weekends in our garage. My parents think it's the coolest thing and got us music from the Beatles plus bands from the 70s and 80s. Oliver has some drum effects on his board, but I really think we could use a live drummer. Maybe you could come over and give it a try one day."

The look on Roadkill's face confirms he thinks I'm out of my mind. Before I can say another word, yard duty announces we can clean up. Kids dump their trash and uneaten food in the garbage can and run to get the best spots in four square and basketball. I stay put, waiting for a response from Roadkill. I give him my best attempt at the "stink eye" I see my grandma give to Grandpa sometimes when she's unhappy with him. It's the look that demands Grandpa do whatever Grandma asks. I borrow her look to make sure Roadkill knows I mean business. He won't leave until I get his answer.

Roadkill stands, holding his empty lunch tray. I hold my breath.

"I'll think about it."

And just like that, he walks away without looking back. I feel like doing a victory dance like the football players after scoring a touchdown. But all I can do is smile.

CHAPTER FIVE

CRAZY IS AS CRAZY DOES

"Are you crazy?" Oliver's loud exclamation causes me to miss my otherwise easy lay-up. We were playing our usual basketball game after being excused.

"You of all people on this planet should know I'm not crazy. If I was, you would be the first to know because of the twin connection we have." I toss the ball to him as Emmanuel joins the game.

"I don't feel twin-connected to you on this one. Emmanuel, can you talk Eddie out of this outrageous idea?"

"What idea?" Emmanuel usually loves my ideas. I knew I could count on his support.

"Pinhead here thinks Roadkill will play drums with us, and we will win the Sun Valley talent search contest." Oliver never calls me by the degrading nickname I'd been tagged with because he knew the name made me feel inferior. I think I've been labeled pinhead by certain kids because of the shape of my head, but mostly because I am intelligent and calling me a derogatory name makes those of lesser brain matter feel smart.

"Are you crazy, Eddie?" Emmanuel sputters, grabs his stomach like it hurts, and falls to the ground in fits of laughter.

"Get up before yard duty thinks there's something wrong with you!" I hold my hand out to Emmanuel, pulling him off the black top.

The RUBBER BAND

"There's no way Roadkill will ever think of hanging out with any of us." Emmanuel brushes the dirt off his clothes. "He's such a loner. I think he carries those drumsticks to keep people from being friendly to him. He probably doesn't even have a drum set to tap a stick on."

"I think you're wrong. I watched him all day Saturday. He was beating out the air drums to whatever he listened to, and I bet if he sits in front of a full drum set, he'll know what to do and never miss a beat." I'm not going to give this idea up. I'm no quitter. Crazy or not, my gut tells me to keep going.

"Doesn't he live at the boy's home? If you go through with this, I think you have to get special permission or something to break him out." Emmanuel is right. I hadn't thought about that part of the equation.

"Maybe, but I think it's worth a try."

"Fine. But I agree with Oliver. You're all capitals crazy!"

We go back to shooting hoops, but I can't help scanning the playground looking for Roadkill. I find him walking the perimeter and playing the air drums like usual.

I don't understand why I feel compelled to do the things I do. Mom says my stubborn spirit and determination will help me make a difference in the world. I don't think I am being stubborn by asking Roadkill to join the band. But maybe I am trying to make a difference in my little corner of the earth. When Roadkill filled my trash bag, he showed me a side hidden from the public. I should feel privileged. Instead, I feel like I'm a mutinous pirate about to walk the plank.

After school, I tell Oliver to go home without me. He doesn't bother asking me why. After my big reveal of the band thing, he knew better not to question my actions. I wait outside the front doors for Roadkill to leave. If he lives at the boy's home, a bus will pick him up, and I'll have my answer. The school door swings open, and Roadkill strolls out tapping his drumsticks to the rhythm of his trotting feet. No van or bus or car waits to pick him up. He keeps walking down the sidewalk with his sticks pounding the air around him.

Where is he going? My curiosity magnetically moves me forward, and I follow him like a stealth fighter, keeping close but out of sight. When he stops to tie his shoe, I duck behind a giant rosebush and get stuck by the thorns. I yelp in pain and almost blow my cover, but quickly whine out my best "hurt dog" impression.

The trick works. Or, maybe his earbuds are playing so loud they tune out sound. No matter, I continue to follow him at a safe, unnoticeable distance.

Five blocks and two left turns later, Roadkill walks up the steps of a two-story house with an enclosed porch, slamming the door behind him. Wait, Roadkill lives in this house? How many times have I walked by on my way home or raced past on my bike and never even noticed the house before? I peek at the house from behind the giant oak tree on the berm.

"Why are you following me, Pinhead?" I almost scurry up the tree like a squirrel when Roadkill's voice booms from behind me. "Answer me, Pinhead." I turn to face him, pressing my back against the bark of the tree.

I can barely breathe as my head spins. My heart pounds against my ribs so hard I think the buttons on my shirt will pop off. "Um, I'm not following you. I'm looking for my brother. Have you seen him?"

Roadkill pokes his drumsticks to my chest.

I'm going to die, impaled by a drumstick through the heart.

"Wait a minute, I saw you go inside. How'd you sneak behind me so fast?"

The RUBBER BAND

"So, you were following me." His sticks press deeper, and I think I hear my ribs pop, but it was just me swallowing hard. "Admit it, Pinhead."

If I do, I am dead. If I don't, I am dead too. Nothing can save me, so I might as well fess up. "Truth is, I wanted to find out if you lived at the boy's home or not."

I am released from death by drumsticks as Roadkill steps away.

"I don't. Now get outta here!"

For some reason, my feet don't cooperate with his demand. "I wanted to know how hard it would be for you to get permission to come over to my house and join our band."

"I don't live in a boy's home. Now scram, Pinhead."

I ease off the tree trunk, dropping my backpack. "Nope. I'm not leaving." I am beginning to agree with Emmanuel and Oliver. I am crazy.

"Whatever." Roadkill ignores me and heads to the house. He isn't getting away that easily.

"Dude. We really need a drummer, and you not living at the boy's home makes joining us easier. I've seen your sense of rhythm. You can hold a beat at the same time as collecting trash. I can't wait to see you behind a drum set."

When Roadkill stops walking, the words stop spilling out of my mouth. He turns to face me as the door opens, and a woman with a baby on her hip calls out, "Rocky, I'm so glad to see you've brought home a friend. Would he like to come inside and have some milk and cookies with us? I baked them fresh today."

I recognize this lady from church. She's always dashing in late and sitting at the back with her husband, but I didn't know she had a baby or that she was Roadkill's mom.

"He was just leaving." Roadkill points a drumstick toward the street.

"Now what kind of friend would turn down my moist, chewy, gooey homemade grandmother's chocolate chip cookie recipe?" The way those words slip out of her mouth made mine drool at the thought of biting into my favorite type of cookie. Add milk to it and it's the best day ever. This nice lady beckons me with her free arm, and much to Roadkill's disapproval, I can't help but be drawn inside. I pick up my backpack in one hand, and with the other, I shake hers.

"Nice to meet you. I'm Edison Taylor, but you can call me Eddie."

"What a fine gentleman you are. I'm Mrs. Perkins, but you can call me Mary. This is my daughter, Rosalinda, but you can call her Rosie for short." Rosie blows a raspberry as Roadkill follows slowly behind.

The house smells like the bakery on main street in the morning. A squeak presses out of a baby toy when I step on it following Mrs. Perkins to the kitchen. She sets the baby in one of those rectangular folding baby pens and reaches into the cupboard.

"You aren't lactose intolerant are you, Eddie?

I am so busy following the tantalizing scent of cookies, I don't notice Roadkill's disappearing act. "No, Mrs. Perkins, I'm not."

"Please, call me Mary, Rocky does." She pours two full glasses of milk and sets a plate of almost steaming, chewy, gooey chocolate chip cookies in front of me as I take my spot at the table.

Wait. Roadkill calls his mom by her first name? How disrespectful is that?

"Okay," I can't help but look at her to make sure it really is okay to call her by her first name, "Mary." She must be afraid of Roadkill too. I take a bite of the warm, moist cookie.

The RUBBER BAND

"Now that's better. I wonder where Rockefeller went. Rocky? I'm pouring you a glass of milk. Come down and be social. He does like to spend time alone, up in his room."

Rockefeller? Who names a kid Rockefeller? Mrs. Perkins must have a thing for names beginning with the letter R, or she is a fan of rich famous people. I'd read about the Rockefellers in a book about New York City. They must've been important because there's an entire center named after them.

Footsteps descend stairs, and Roadkill appears without his drumsticks.

He pulls out a chair to sit across the table from me with a blank stare on his face.

"Eddie, I know your parents. Your dad, Dr. Fred Taylor, delivered my Rosie, and I love your mom's art studio. One day when Rosie is older, I'd love for her to take the art classes your mom offers. It's so nice of Rocky to bring you over."

As she went on and on about how wonderful my family is, I could see Roadkill stuffing cookies in his mouth and gulping down the milk. He got a white mustache from the backsplash but wipes his mouth on his shirt sleeve, clinking his glass on the table as I take my last swallow.

"Those were the best cookies I've had since Christmas, but I better get going. I usually go straight home, and Mom might be worried."

"Yeah, you better get home." Roadkill reaches for another cookie.

Mary frowns at Roadkill's words. "You're welcome to stop by any time you want to hang out with Rocky. I can't promise I'll have fresh cookies, but I'm sure there'll be something to share. I know how hungry kids can get after a long day at school."

Opening the front door, I turn to say thank you and ask a question. "Mary, I was wondering if Road, um, Rocky might be able to come over to my house after school and play the drums in my garage band?" I'm not patient enough to wait for an answer from Roadkill. The clock is ticking, and time is running out to enter and prepare for the talent search contest. He certainly can't back out now. His sweet cookie-baking mom won't want him to miss out on the socializing that I sincerely believe he needs.

Roadkill's face turns blood red, and I picture the drumsticks pressing through my skin, past my ribs, and into my heart, stirring it to hamburger meat.

"Since I know your parents, I don't have a problem with Rocky spending time at your house. I'll have to discuss this with my husband when he gets home. Why don't I call your mom later, so we can talk about it?"

Roadkill disappears up the stairs.

"Okay." The deal is pretty much sealed. I can't wait to celebrate but won't run or do any shouting for joy until I'm totally out of her view.

As I head down the sidewalk, Mary asks one last question.

"Do you have a drum set for him to play? He has the sticks, but we haven't been able to find an affordable set."

Every tingle of joy turns off like I blew a spark plug in my happiness motor. Roadkill has drumsticks with him all the time. I never thought he didn't have a drum to use them on. I offer her a weak "Of course." A half lie, or little white lie because after all, technically we do have a drum set on Oliver's electric piano. The computerized drum sound didn't require sticks.

CHAPTER SIX

CARL'S LIST

My feet don't keep up with my mind, racing with ideas. I nearly trip over my untied shoelace. I can't wait to get home and don't take time to stop to tie my shoelace. Time is something I don't have enough of when it comes to my mission. I bound up the front steps and fly through the front door straight to the desk in my room. The rule is I can't do anything until my homework is done.

"I'm so glad to see you enthusiastic about getting your work done." Mom leans against the door frame. Her folded arms are spattered with various colored paint drops. "If I didn't know any better, I'd say you have something more important you need to do."

I never could hide anything from my mom. Without hesitation, I make my request known. "Can I get a drum set?"

Mom's face wrinkles like a grape turning into a raisin. "Why do you suddenly need a drum set when Oliver's keyboard has an electronic sound for one? That was one reason we got it for him, so the two of you could create all kinds of music together."

Just then Oliver shows up munching on a granola bar, dragging his backpack behind him. He freezes in his tracks hearing my request. His mouth gapes so wide open, bits of granola drop on the carpet.

The RUBBER BAND

I want to explain my mission to Mom but don't want to do it twice and decide to wait until dinner, so I can get Dad's immediate support. He loves helping others. I guess that's why he became a doctor. I'll give Mom some teaser information to make her curious, then at dinner, when I have a captive audience with mouthfuls of food, I'll tell them my plans. That way if their mouths drop open with surprise, they won't have to vacuum the floor when food falls out.

"Remember how you and Dad always tell us to set goals and work toward achieving them?"

"Of course, I do." She drops her arms to her sides and smiles.

"I have a goal involving a real drum set. The kind with high hat cymbals, snares, and a bass drum with a kick pedal."

Oliver continues chewing the rest of his granola bar.

"I like that you have plans and goals, but this sounds like something we need to talk about with Daddy at dinner."

I can't agree with her more.

"Have you had a snack yet? You look famished." I don't have the courage to tell her about Mrs. Perkins's ooey, gooey, chocolate chip cookies. But this way I can get my hands on another snack, and after running home, I deserve to eat more treats.

Once I have my second snack in less than an hour in my hands and on its way to my mouth, I return to find Oliver sitting backwards, chest pressing against his desk chair, thumping his feet on the floor to whatever he was listening to on his headset. I ignore him and get to work at my desk.

"Where did you disappear after school?" I recognize a Beatles' tune coming from his now pulled-off earphones.

"Nowhere," I answer while completing the first math problem.

"We always walk home together. What do you think you were doing following Rocky?"

I swivel around to sit in my chair backwards like Oliver. "You followed me?"

"Did you really think whining like a dog would fool Roadkill? Of course, I followed you. After your big announcement today, I knew you were up to something and got worried. But when Mrs. Perkins answered the door, and I smelled the cookies, I figured you'd tell me everything when you got home. You didn't happen to bring home one of those cookies to share, did you?"

"If I had one more of Mrs. Perkins's ooey, gooey, fresh-from-the-oven cookies, I'd have eaten it by now. They were the best chocolate chip cookies I've ever had."

"Better than Mom's?"

"Oh, yeah." I lick my lips thinking of Mrs. Perkins's delicious cookies. "But don't tell Mom I said so. I don't want to hurt her feelings."

"Are you going to tell me what you're up to?"

I turn back to my homework. "You can wait until dinner." A pillow hits the back of my head. He isn't going to get away with me ignoring his pillow fight challenge. I grab my pillow from the bed and retaliate. Good thing we don't have downy pillows. With our hardy fights, it might snow feathers in our room.

Scents of baked ham with gravy and crunchy onion, green bean casserole waft through the heater vents into my room causing my stomach to grumble. After Oliver gives up, and I win the pillow fight, I set back to finishing my homework then write up a plan to get a band together to win the Sun Valley talent search contest. With family dinner minutes away, I can't tell if the butterflies flitting about in my stomach are from excitement or hunger. Either way, they'd stop flying around soon enough.

The RUBBER BAND

I love dinner time with my family. We talk and laugh, and when we are done eating, we sit back and take turns answering two questions: 1) What was the best thing that happened to you today? and 2) Is there something you would do differently?

As I stuff a second helping of savory green bean casserole into my mouth, I contemplate my answers. Family dinner is the perfect setup to reveal my plan.

"So, Oliver," my dad pushes his plate away and leans back in his chair. "What was the best thing that happened to you today?"

"Why don't you ask Eddie first."

I choke on the green beans causing Mom to jump up, ready to give me the Heimlich maneuver. All eyes are on me as I take a long drink of water, washing my half-chewed food down my throat. I have their undivided attention.

"The best thing that happened to me today was I followed Rocky Espinosa home and found out he doesn't live in the boy's home but actually has a mom and little baby sister."

No one said a word. They seem to be frozen in time like in the movies when everything stops except the main character, and he gets to walk around poking at all the raindrops suspended in midair. Since I'm the main character, it's time to poke at some raindrops. I take a deep breath as words uncontrollably spill out my mouth, revealing my plan.

"I want to enter a band in the Sun Valley talent search contest. We already have most of the players but need a drummer, and since Road—" I correct myself, "Rocky is always carrying his drumsticks around, I followed him home to ask if he would play drums with us."

From the looks on their faces, I need to explain more.

"We have Emmanuel on bass guitar, me on the lead, Oliver on keyboard, and Rocky would be our drummer, only he doesn't have a drum set, so we would have to find one." The excitement of telling my story was spilling out so quickly I almost forget to breathe. I pause for air long enough for my dad to speak.

"Eddie, what a fabulous idea."

I don't get to reveal my complete plan, but I see the wheels spinning in my dad's brain from across the table. He loves projects, and with him helping, Oliver can't have any objections. He'd have to play keyboards for the band.

"Is there any way we can find a drum set, so Rocky can come over?" Oliver's glare after my comment felt like he was hitting me with more than a pillow. Instead, he hit me with words, blurting his feelings out.

"I can't believe you want to invite Roadkill over. He's a mean, scary bully, always in Principal Haymaker's office in trouble. You can't possibly think he'd want to hang out with us and enter a talent contest. He's not the kind of person to call our friend. I don't think he knows how to be a friend from the way he acts."

We always know when something we say causes our parents to go into a state of shock. They get really quiet, and their faces, well, let's just say their faces look like they would if I said a bad word.

The only noise we can hear is the refrigerator making ice. Since Oliver's comments make the room stand still, I can't wait to hear what my dad has to say.

"Oliver, do you know what the phrase 'don't judge a book by its cover' means?"

When Dad starts a conversation with a question followed by a cliché phrase, or technically an idiom, we know we aren't in trouble. Instead, we'd be hearing a lecture on how to better our eight-year-old lives.

The RUBBER BAND

"Rockefeller Espinosa is in foster care living with the Perkins temporarily. He never had a family to come home to or to experience the privilege both of you have grown up with, so it's no wonder he's closed off and protective of himself. He's had no one to take care of him. He's just a lost young boy who needs extra care. So, you see, he may be all hard and dark on the outside, but on the inside, he's soft and hoping for a light to shine on his dreams."

My head spins circles around this new revelation. Roadkill Rocky is soft on the inside? Mrs. Perkins isn't his mom, and little Rosie isn't his baby sister? For future reference, I need to get my facts straight.

Dad keeps talking even though my mind is swirling. "No one knows the story of his real family, but he's in good hands with the Perkinses for now. Maybe inviting him over on a regular basis would show him how to be a true friend. Kids in the foster care system need stability, understanding, and love."

Dad is onto something. I don't know if I could actually love Roadkill, but I certainly am beginning to understand him better. Dad's words aren't a lecture, but a truth we needed to hear. Rocky doesn't have a family of his own. No wonder he keeps to himself. He doesn't have anyone to trust.

"How about I check Carl's List online for used musical instruments for sale and find Rocky an affordable drum set to get started? Maybe after a trial run, we can see if everyone is up to entering the band in the Sun Valley contest."

Dad is always a forward thinker. He's got me using one of his phrases to describe him, "grass never grows under his feet." I guess I'm just a chip off the old block.

CHAPTER SEVEN

STACKED HANDS

As soon as dinner is finished, we gather around Dad's computer as he opens up Carl's List, immediately locating several used drum sets. There are many listings for drums in various conditions. I like the looks of one with a scratchy silver shine design. Dad says it's not the color that matters but the quality. The silver scratchy design set is manufactured in China and is a stock photo, so the picture isn't really of what we'd be buying. I trust my dad's judgment. After all, he's going to be the one paying for the drum set, so I really don't have much choice in the matter.

"This looks like a good one." Dad points out a five-piece set in the coolest shade of blue. I like the silvery-grey set from my online search at school, but this set's color shines like midnight stars.

"I like it! Oliver, what do you think?"

I can tell Oliver isn't sold on the band idea by his not-so-enthusiastic response.

"It's blue," he says, leaning over Dad's shoulder.

"Color doesn't matter, it's the quality, right Dad?"

"The price is within reason. If it's still available, I think we should have Rocky come with us to try the set out." Dad's plan sounds great to me. Oliver doesn't say a word. "If I hear from the seller tonight, I'll talk with Mrs. Perkins about bringing Rocky, and maybe we can pick it up tomorrow."

The RUBBER BAND

Dad's always been a man of quick action. The date of the talent search contest is another day closer, and I don't have a complete band yet. If my plan is going to work, things need to happen faster than the Flash can run, and I'm pretty sure nothing outruns him.

I find out at breakfast Dad got called in the middle of the night to deliver a baby for one of his patients, so I go to school without knowing if we have a drum set appointment or not. How can I concentrate at school when there's an idea as huge as the Pacific Ocean sloshing about in my mind?

At morning recess, instead of meeting the guys on the basketball courts, I escape to the library computer and Google drum sets. Within fifteen minutes, I memorize the anatomy of a basic drum kit, complete with variations of sticks and cymbals, preparing to be the best drum scout ever. The shiny greyish silver sets still look the best to me.

As we settle in for the second half of our morning's education, both Oliver and Emmanuel stare me down. Oliver whispers, "Where did you disappear to?" I don't have time to answer since Miss Crenshaw is already passing out the literature assignments. Maybe I'll get a chance to tell him when we go to our writing centers.

Well, that isn't going to happen. Miss Crenshaw keeps us so busy, before my stomach can growl, we are being dismissed for lunch.

Racing to our usual table with a scolding from yard duty to slow down, Oliver and Emmanuel demand an immediate explanation to my whereabouts at morning recess.

"I needed to do some research, so I was in the library."

"What for? Miss Crenshaw hasn't assigned any big projects." A drop of grape jelly oozes out of Emmanuel's PBJ as he chomps into it.

"Do you know a drum set can have two bass drums with kicks?"

"I know what he was doing." Oliver snickers. "He was checking out drums because he asked Roadkill to play drums with us. Only Roadkill doesn't really have a drum set to play on, so Eddie asks our dad to buy him one, so we can practice in our garage every day after school."

Emmanuel stops chewing as Oliver continues.

"I told him it was a bad idea. But, when he brought the subject up at dinner to our dad, and Dad loved the idea, I'm afraid there is no backing out now."

"Roadkill is never without drumsticks, so he must know how to play, right?" Emmanuel adds his thoughts without objecting, so I think he might approve, but I hadn't officially asked Emmanuel to join the band adventure yet either.

"Eddie thinks Roadkill has a good sense of rhythm after watching him drum his sticks while filling bags of trash at the community service workday." Oliver rubs in the fact his well-behaved brother had gotten in big trouble.

"Look, guys, we have a lot of fun fooling around with music in our garage, playing old stuff, and just free-styling, but I think it's time we do something else. I haven't signed us up for the contest yet, and we don't know if Rocky can really play drums. If we find out he can, then let's agree to give it a try. What could it hurt?"

I know they are thinking about the idea because they are chewing their food really fast, so they can talk. Emmanuel is the first to swallow.

"Roadkill can't hurt us with adults around, but if we do one thing to cross him, we're his next road-pizza."

The RUBBER BAND

"Does that mean you guys are in?" I put my hand flat out on the table, waiting for them to stack theirs on mine.

Emmanuel's hand is the first to stack. "I'm in."

Oliver puts his sandwich back in his lunchbox and stacks his hand on top of Emmanuel's. "I don't have much choice. I'm in too."

"AWESOME!" I think the whole school hears me because yard duty walks toward our table like we are in for a scolding, and the kids at the next table over became silent statues with food hanging out of their mouths.

We raise our stacked hands in quiet victory, so we won't attract more attention. Emmanuel wipes some wayward mayonnaise from his hand, no doubt off my brother's slathered sandwich.

"Eww, gross. How can you stand this white goo on your sandwich?" he says in a not-so-happy voice.

"Dude, I like my food extra moist and juicy." Oliver's messy face is proof.

"Well, that doesn't mean you have to share it with everyone. Eddie, didn't your mom teach you guys simple manners like wiping your face, not on your sleeve but with a napkin?"

I toss Oliver the napkin Mom had packed in my lunch box.

"Yes, she did, but we don't always follow directions." Oliver gives his face a once-over with the paper towel. I don't care if my brother is messy. I just need him to play the keyboard.

Yard duty starts to dismiss tables. As we dash off to the basketball court, I notice Rocky with his headset, walking his usual route on the perimeter of the school yard, and I smile. Something deep within my young heart tells me this is the best idea I've ever come up with.

CHAPTER EIGHT

Wow–Just WOW!

I learned to tell time before first grade. Right now, I wish I could speed the hands on the clock, so the dismissal bell will ring, and I can rush home. I'm not able to concentrate after lunch. Good thing all we have is art and PE to help me pass the time. I get really crazy on creating a Picasso face of myself in art, and score a goal in soccer, the highlights of my afternoon. But the clock doesn't move any faster.

Miss Crenshaw is reading to us from a chapter book for the last fifteen minutes of class when the phone rings. Whispering always starts when she answers the phone. The whispering rolls into a low rumble before I hear her say, "Thank you, I'll let them know."

Miss Crenshaw gives us the "quiet coyote" sign with her fingers, but since it's close to when class is over and it's time to go home, we get antsy and don't listen. She starts the count down. We lose class points if we aren't quiet before she gets to zero. When we reach twenty-five reward points, we get a class party.

"Four, three, two," Miss Crenshaw folds a finger down on her hand for each number. I guess we don't want her to fold her thumb down and lose points because we get quiet, fast. "Eddie and Oliver, your dad will be picking you up after school so don't walk home, okay, boys? Emmanuel, you're going with them."

The RUBBER BAND

Oliver looks at me with a wrinkled mouth. I'm confused too. We always walk home. In unison, we reply, "Okay."

I don't hear the rest of the chapter Miss Crenshaw reads. Why is Dad picking us up? Had something terrible happened to Mom, so she won't be there when we get home? I hope the reason isn't a dentist appointment. I hate going to the dentist. He always pokes around in places you don't reach with your toothbrush and finds cavities.

Before I can think of other awful things, I remember the drum set. I can barely stay in my seat for the excitement raising my heart rate. I eyeball the clock. Just five more minutes until the bell rings.

Miss Crenshaw closes the book and dismisses us by our magic numbers to pack up. I'm seventeen, and Oliver is eighteen, so we meet at our cubbies. While stuffing our backpacks, we wonder why Dad is coming to get us.

"I'm pretty sure we're going to the see the dentist. I saw the appointment on the refrigerator calendar in bold print. My teeth are hurting just thinking about it." Oliver voices his concerns before I can tell him what I think.

"Nope, not even close. Did you forget Dad's plan about the drums?"

"You guys worry too much," Emmanuel interrupts, reaching into his cubby. "It's probably nothing."

"I'm pretty sure it's about the drums. Why else would Emmanuel be coming home with us?"

Becca pushes Emmanuel out of her way, grabbing books from her cubby.

"Hey, watch it, Becca." Emmanuel rubs his arm.

"Yeah, watch it, Becca." I reach into my cubby for my backpack.

"You guys take too long. I've got to get to homecoming practice, so I can sing the National Anthem perfectly."

The three of us back out of her way as she tromps to the head of the line.

"Perfect, schmerfect. All she thinks of is herself. So, what if she can sing? I bet she chokes on the high-note ending in front of all those people this weekend." I zip my bag up and sling it over my shoulder.

"That would be humiliating, and I'd like to see it," Oliver adds.

"Me too," Emmanuel says, "but I'll be at my grandma's house this weekend. I'll have to hear about it from you guys."

"I'm sure Bossy Becca will let the entire class know how she did, even if she hits a sour note or two."

We join the back of the line as Miss Crenshaw walks us down the hallway to the front door. Our van is first in line to pick up. Dad waves, and the side door opens. Oliver, Emmanuel, and I freeze like statues.

"Come on guys, get in," Dad beckons, but we don't move. In the back seat, giving us the evil snake eye, sits Roadkill.

This is definitely about the drum set.

We pile in without as much as a grunt. Emmanuel takes the seat behind Dad, and Oliver sits next to him. I have to crawl over Oliver to get to the back, and unfortunately, I trip over the seat buckle on Oliver's chair, falling face first next to Roadkill. He snorts out a snicker. Heat rushes to my head as I scramble to the corner as far away from Roadkill as I can before fastening my seatbelt. No one speaks as Dad drives off.

I stare at the back of Oliver's and Emmanuel's heads, hoping Dad will say something to ease the uncomfortable silence in the back of the van. For one second, I dare to sneak a peek at Roadkill. He is thumping his fingers to a tune coming from his earbuds I can almost recognize.

I know we were all thinking it, but Oliver decides to ask, so we know for sure.

The RUBBER BAND

"Where are WE going, Dad?"

"You'll find out soon enough." Dad drives down the street to the highway and turns toward Santa Rosa. We do most of our shopping and appointments like my dentist there, but I know this isn't about any of that.

Watching the clock on the dashboard makes time pass slowly. Dad said last night we might take Roadkill with us to look at a drum set, but sitting next to Roadkill in the backseat of our van with my two best friends in front of me not speaking makes the suspense worse. Dad sings along to a tune on the radio without telling us why we're all together. I know why, but when Dad pulls into the supermarket parking lot, I'm not so sure anymore.

"Okay guys, pile out and follow me." Dad's voice has a sort of musical jingle to it.

I let Roadkill leave first, so I can keep an eye on him.

"I know you guys are wondering what's up." The van lock chirps behind us as we follow Dad to a store I have never noticed before, Arnie's Second-Hand Music.

"I got special permission from all adults to bring you here." Dad opens the door and ushers us in.

A thin man with curly hair and a scraggly beard reaches to shake Dad's hand.

"Hello, I'm Dr. Taylor, and you must be Arnie. We spoke earlier on the phone about the thing you have on hold for me in the back room."

"Yes, I've been waiting for you. I've already had a couple of calls regarding the 'thing' but held it for you since you explained the special circumstances. I hope it's what you're looking for." We follow as Arnie leads us to the back of the store into a small warehouse.

I stay back behind everyone, keeping my eye on Roadkill. I know we're in the presence of adults, but I don't trust him.

At any minute, he could turn on me and pound me with the drumsticks poking out of his back pocket.

"Here it is. Isn't she beautiful?" Arnie holds his arm out like he's introducing us to someone. I nearly bump into everyone as they form a wall barricading me. I push my way through to see what stopped them.

"It's practically brand new. The owner bought it for his kid, but the kid decided to get into motocross instead, and it was taking up too much space. I guess they needed the garage for all the mechanical things involved in dirt bike racing." I don't hear much of what Arnie says after that. I can't even speak. In front of my eyes is the blue drum set we had seen on Carl's List last night, perfectly set up and ready to play.

"Go ahead, Rocky," Dad says. "Give it a try."

For a moment, Roadkill hesitates. His eyes dart from the drum set to my dad and back. I hold my breath as Roadkill slowly pulls his drumsticks from his back jeans pocket and makes his way to the stool behind the drums. He sits down, puts in his earbuds, presses play, and just like that, his arms set in motion a great rhythm. Our jaws drop. We don't even know what tune he is drumming to. He lays down a beat so amazing, I know the band has a drummer.

Dad taps his foot to the rhythm while the three of us gawk in amazement.

Seems like the world is revolving around Roadkill. He jams until beads of sweat trickle down his forehead. I imagine a fog machine blowing smoke, filling the air with a misty haze. Colored laser lights flash while Roadkill plays his drum solo. A crowd is rushing the stage chanting "Roadkill, Roadkill, Roadkill," and security pushes against crazy fans attempting to crawl on stage.

I'm brought back to reality by a smaller audience's applause as Roadkill holds his drumsticks in the air, shouting, "YES!"

Dad looks at Arnie and says, "We'll take it."

The RUBBER BAND

We do some rearranging, and Roadkill has to sit up front with Dad, but we leave Arnie's store with a five-piece, pearly blue drum set packed in the van.

Getting the drum set happened so fast, I feel like I am still dreaming of the hazy concert stage. But as the van turns onto the highway and heads back to Wildwood, I can't help but smile to myself.

I was right. Roadkill can play a real drum set. Wow! Just WOW!

CHAPTER NINE

Questions

The only noise on the drive home comes from the radio playing oldies. I think all of us are still in shock by what has happened in such a short period of time. All I can think about is now Roadkill has no choice but to join the band. He has to play drums with us. I thought Dad was going to drive Emmanuel and Rocky home, but instead, we pull into our driveway.

"What kind of pizza do you guys like? I'm going to have Joey's deliver. I got a drum set to put together, and I don't want Mom to worry about four hungry boys." Dad always has a plan.

We settle for pepperoni and cheese with a side of cheesy breadsticks.

Dad had arranged for Emmanuel's mom to drop off his guitar and amplifier. While he sets up the drums, Oliver, Emmanuel, and I warm up on our guitars and keyboard. We always tinker around before we start to play something organized, like an orchestra waiting for the conductor. Roadkill leans against our washing machine, arms folded with drumsticks at the ready.

The doorbell chimes, and we rush to the kitchen. Mom takes out paper plates for us to stack piles of extra-large slices of steaming, cheesy, pepperoni goodness. She pours four tall glasses of lemonade. Three of us help ourselves without a care

The RUBBER BAND

and head back to the garage, but Roadkill doesn't touch a slice. I pause before joining my pals. Roadkill is speaking to my mom, and I want to hear what he has to say.

"Thank you for the pizza, Mrs. Taylor."

I almost drop my full plate of pizza but catch it before my pizza has a chance to hit the floor.

"You're so welcome, Rocky. It's nice to have you as our guest." Mom hands him a plate, and he takes one slice. "Is that all you're going to have? I know you're hungrier than that." She insists, and even I know better not to turn Mom down when she means business. He grabs another slice of pepperoni but not before Mom can add, "Don't forget your drink."

As he takes the glass, I slip into the garage. There's no way I want Roadkill to know I caught him being polite.

Roadkill walks in just as Dad finishes putting the last drum in place. Roadkill takes one bite of pizza and sets his plate on the dryer. When he sits down, the stool behind the set made the same whooshing sound as the chair outside Mr. Haymaker's office. Roadkill's drumsticks hit each piece of the set once, bouncing sound waves of percussion off the walls and getting our attention, and then he flies into a personal solo, causing dust to come down from the rafters.

Dad's smile seems a mile wide, watching Roadkill rock out. My heart hits my rib cage with every pound of the bass drum. I can't wait to get on my guitar and play along, but why let a good slice of pizza get cold? I finish my slice first. I think Oliver and Emmanuel feel the same way. We are having our own personal dinner and show. A miracle was happening before our eyes and in my garage watching Roadkill play something other than air drums.

Dad gets Roadkill's attention, and he rests his drumsticks on the snare. Roadkill looks like he didn't want to stop.

"I promised your moms I'd have you home by eight, so we're running out of time. I'm going to go and sign your band up for the contest. Maybe you can use this time to talk about practicing and set a schedule?"

I'd totally forgotten. In order to be good enough to get anywhere with the contest, a lot of practice will be required. That means we'll have to spend many afternoons and weekends hanging out with Roadkill. Reality is setting in, and even though I love my plan, I am beginning to think I've lost all my senses.

Emmanuel snaps us into a conversation by asking the first question.

"How about we practice after school for at least an hour? That should be enough time to master one tune before the contest."

"Well, since Dad is at this very moment making our official entry, we need to get something together sooner than later," Oliver adds.

I can't believe this is actually happening.

Roadkill doesn't say a word, but I can feel his steely eyes giving me a stare. He gets much farther with his frowny "I'm a big bully don't mess with me" look than he does with words.

Strapping on my guitar, I face the guys. They are right. We have to audition for the contest, so we need to pick a song and practice it to perfection in order to be considered for the final cut. My plan is coming together so fast, my brain starts sloshing around in my skull. There is too much to think about, and I can't get anything straight except that we have a band of four guys who have never played together, trying to make decisions based on my crazy idea hatched while I was in trouble sitting in Principal Haymaker's office.

I must have zoned out into my own worried little world because I think I hear Roadkill say something about food.

The RUBBER BAND

"Let's just jam." Roadkill picks up his sticks and starts a beat. Oliver wipes his greasy fingers on his jeans and takes to the keyboard. Emmanuel gets his bass guitar playing a basic beat. I pluck on the strings, strumming out the first thing that comes to my mind.

Just like that, a miracle happens.

We are making our own music, and we actually sound pretty good. There is no rhyme or reason to the music. We are jamming, like magic.

I don't think I've seen Roadkill smile before.

If he could only see how much happiness beams from his face. I feel my face doing the same thing. Happiness floods me from head to toe as goosebumps flock up my arms. My dream of winning the contest seems possible, especially with Roadkill's talent.

The music comes to an abrupt stop as Dad returns waving his hands to get us to quiet down. "Congratulations! You're officially a youth band."

Dad holds out the printed entry form.

"There are a lot of things you boys need to decide as soon as possible," he says in his serious doctor voice. "The first thing will be to pick one tune and practice it to near perfection. I don't have to register what you are playing, but I think the sooner you choose, the better. We can make a recording and send our official audition in digitally. But right now, it's close to eight, and I do need to get Emmanuel and Rocky home, so, pack up, gentlemen."

Dad has no idea what he started.

"Dad's right. We need to play a classic awesome rock 'n' roll song. One the audience will recognize. That way when we nail-it, they will love us instantly." I can't help but spill a bit of my daydreams about our success. The guys' foreheads crinkle up like they are thinking about what I just said. I'm serious about winning. I want to win now more than ever.

"We could do one of the Beatles' tunes we fool around with." Emmanuel puts his guitar on its stand. "I think the easiest for us would be the 'Yellow Submarine.' It's slower, and we could master it quickly."

"I don't want us to sound easy. I want to sound fantastic! I want us to overwhelm the audience with our amazing style, be unforgettable, so unforgettable they will want an encore." There's no way I'll agree for my plan to go the easy way. There never is an easy way if you want to be the best.

My comment sparks a round of arguing protests between Oliver, Emmanuel, and I, all out of turn, talking at once, increasing in volume in out-of-control decibels.

Rimshot!

We freeze like ice sculptures.

"We'll never get anywhere if you three keep arguing." Roadkill glares at us like the piercing laser in a light game hitting the chest target, eliminating the player. We stand in shock when Roadkill speaks—it's usually an insult or threat.

"How about we each choose three tunes to play, and when we get together tomorrow, vote on one?" When Roadkill speaks, it's usually an insult or threat. "We have a huge problem."

The three of us gather around the kid everyone fears, not muttering a sound.

What problem? I don't see one. The only problem is us guys are afraid of Roadkill.

Roadkill tucks his drumsticks in his back jean pocket. "Look guys, we can practice any tune to perfection, but without vocals, we're just another boring instrumental group."

The last thing I want us to be is boring.

"We need a lead singer," Roadkill adds.

Of course, Roadkill is brilliant! Why I didn't I think of that?

The RUBBER BAND

"Road—Rocky's right. But who do we know that can sing and is willing to join us?" Oliver's words seem to make him wholeheartedly in on the plan.

"We'd definitely sound better with someone singing." Emmanuel sets his bass in its case.

Another big crazy idea suddenly comes to my mind. Before I can make any sense of my thoughts, I open my mouth. "I know someone. In fact, this person is used to being in the spotlight and might be our only choice at this point."

Silent eyes stare at me.

"Let's ask Becca."

I stand there like I'm in the underwear dream where you're in front of the class and forgot to get dressed that morning. Everyone is laughing at you. But at that moment in my garage, no one is laughing, especially Emmanuel and Oliver, and I am fully clothed.

"Who's Becca?" Roadkill's voice breaks the silence.

Oliver hit the keyboards in a minor tone like the ones you hear in old movies when Dracula appears. Having watched Rocky play the drums so well, my fear of him turns to boldness as I give him the lowdown on Bossy Becca.

"She's in our class and can sing the National Anthem like she's on that TV show where everyone sings in front of three judges. I think she'd get the golden buzzer and make it to the final show on her first try." I can't believe I speak so nicely about Bossy Becca. Despite her mean spirit, she has more wind in her lungs than a hurricane pounding the Florida coast. Besides, she is the only person I know who can sing.

"No way. We call her 'Bossy Becca' for a reason. There's got to be someone else." Oliver tosses his opinion out. I know deep down in his heart Emmanuel agrees with Oliver but remains quiet.

"Look, guys, we don't have a lot of time to do try-outs for a singer. Everyone has heard her sing, except for Road …"

I almost call him by the name everyone at school calls him. But I catch myself just in time, saving my life. "R-r-rocky."

Before I can see if I'm in Rocky's line-of-sight for his "I'm going to squash you look," Oliver and Emmanuel try to out-do each other in the comment department.

"She's the grumpiest kid in class and never smiles unless she's talking about herself." Oliver grumbles.

"Yeah, I always let her win if we end up playing math games together. She's a sore loser and will go into rage mode if she doesn't get her way."

I could add my Bossy Becca stories to the pile, but Oliver and Emmanuel keep bantering back and forth.

"Becca is so mean, she's like a fire-breathing dragon just waiting to burn you up and dance in your ashes." Oliver stomps his foot like he's smashing a bug.

"If you cut off her dragon head, just like they say, two more will grow back!"

"There's no way I want a dragon as our lead singer."

Their voices grow louder with every sentence as if they are trying to bust through the roof. If I don't stop them, Dad might come out and end it, immediately. Dad is pretty good at intervention, but I think we can solve this one on our own. I'm about to get between them when Roadkill takes charge.

Rimshot!

"No one is going to win anything if we can't get along. Eddie started this band. If he says this 'Bossy Becca' can sing, then, she can sing."

Who's gonna argue with Road—I mean Rocky? He doesn't say much, but when he does, I listen.

CHAPTER TEN

Answers

In bed, I fight sleep. I toss, turn, and roll my blanket coverings into tornado knots. The guys left it up to me to ask Becca to join us. Now, instead of trying to drift into dreamland, all I can do is worry through every plan I can come up with to convince her. Trying to sleep, I count imaginary sheep. I never understood how people did that or even why, so I turn the sheep into a band, playing in my garage. That only made me laugh. I can't tell you when I finally fall asleep, but I sleep long enough to have a nightmare …

… The door to the third grade room looms in front of me like a well-worn giant armored gate at the end of a drawbridge—the kind you don't want to cross because the evil king and his band of ruthless warriors are waiting to capture and kill you. Extra-large iron hinges creak as I strain to pull the door open to the inky blackness of the unlit room. My feet drag like cement blocks scratching lines across the freshly shined linoleum floor. I move in slow motion toward the book nook corner full of giant beanbag chairs. A quiet hum like the drum roll at the beginning of "The Star-Spangled Banner" flows from underneath the multi-colored beanbags. As my heavy feet drag, inching me closer to the pile, the familiar singing voice of Bossy Becca stops my forward motion. I try to speak, but words stockpile in my throat, and I choke, spewing them out over my swollen tongue, making no sense at all. My feet cement to the floor. I stand a vulnerable statue.

Then the singing turns to lyrics I can understand. "Oh, say can you see by the dawn's early light." Becca's beautiful voice rings out as the morning sun begins to peek through the blinds shining on the pile. The motionless beanbags take a form resembling Godzilla, come alive, and move toward my cemented body. The monster's mouth full of ginormous teeth set to eat me in a single snap, but not before the lyrics bellow from deep within its stuffed body. The voice skips some bars and jumps straight to: "And the rocket's red glare, the bombs bursting in air," belching out fireworks shooting up through the classroom's ceiling, breaking into the dark sky above in flower shapes of sizzling rainbow colors. I glare upward at the patriotic display, but something pulls my head downward.

The music continues to increase as sound waves flow from the giant beanbag lizard giving freedom and life to the notes as they jump from the bars of the sheet music. They fly toward me like bats from a cave, circling, joining hands, and dancing around me, mocking in perfect crescendo.

Pinhead! Pinhead! Pinhead!

The notes become gigantic anthropomorphic beings closing in on me, tightening the circle, clouding my sight of the beanbag lizard while keeping up their taunting like an army drill chant. I fight for air as the half notes play their way up my arm and twist around my neck. Quarter notes tap in unison at my ears while a string of eighth notes cuff my hands and ankles.

With no strength to fight back, I crumble to my knees. The notes will be the end of me. But then, like the moment of suspense in a movie, when you think all is over for the good guy but suddenly hope comes busting through, I can see a ray of sunshine through the darkness. Bossy Becca's face attached to the head of the beanbag lizard explodes through the note-circle to rescue me. She bellows in perfect key,

"O'er the land of the free and the home of the brave…"

"I'm brave! I'm brave!" I open my eyes to Oliver shaking my shoulders.

"Eddie, wake up!"

I grab Oliver, squeezing him tight to my chest.

"Thank goodness it's you and not beanbag Godzilla."

"What?" Oliver wiggles out of my squeeze.

"I just had one of those weird morphing dreams where I was about to be swallowed up by a strangling cluster of notes but was saved just in time by a beanbag lizard with a strange resemblance to Becca."

Arriving early to school that morning, I go straight to the library, find myself a quiet corner, hide behind an extra-large picture book where I can watch the clock tick seconds away, wishing time would slow down for once. I don't want to talk to anyone. I've already been hassled enough at breakfast by Oliver over last night's dream. He nagged at me about when I will talk to Becca. The bell chimes announcing time for me to go through with my nightmare-causing, sleep-losing, thought-about-too-much plan.

I rush through our routine of math warm-up, grab a stack of cards, and set up for a game with Becca, certain she'll be my partner. Emmanuel plops down in front of me.

"What are you doing?" I give him Grandma's snake-eye look.

"I finished my math, so here I am to play Top-It with you."

The RUBBER BAND

"NO! That's not the plan." I scan the room to find Becca. She is chewing the eraser on her pencil, and it doesn't look like she'll be finished with her math warm-up any time soon. It figures. The one day I need Becca to finish fast like she always does, she sits at her desk like she's stumped.

"What plan? You know the rules about playing with the person who finishes next. That's me, your best friend. So, let's play."

"As much as I would normally want to be paired with you, I need to play with Becca, so I can talk to her about singing for the band. Now, you've gone and ruined the best chance I had, especially after I was almost strangled by musical notes and eaten by a beanbag monster."

Before Emmanuel can question my freaky, weird story, Miss Crenshaw calls him to her desk. I know he isn't in trouble. In fact, I hope he's totally messed up on his warm-up math because that means he'll go back to his desk to correct it, and I'll have another shot at playing with Becca. Miss Crenshaw whispers to Emmanuel while pointing out a few things with her pencil.

Behind my back, I cross my fingers. I'm not superstitious, but I have seen other kids cross their fingers when they are hoping for something good to happen, so I thought it can't hurt to try. If Emmanuel got one problem wrong, Miss Crenshaw will help him get the correct answer at her desk. But, if he's got wrong answers on more than one, he'll go back to his desk to redo them, and Becca will be my partner. I cross my fingers tighter, close my eyes, and make my wish.

I open one eye to see Emmanuel return to his desk. I'm about to celebrate my wish coming true as Becca stands from her back-row desk to take her work to Miss Crenshaw. But, out of nowhere, Rowan Parks, who sits a few desks ahead of Becca, grabs his paper and heads to the front.

Time for intervention.

"Rowan, your shoes are untied." I lie. But I know Rowan is the kind of kid who worries about his buttons being in the right holes and whether his socks match his T-shirt. If he felt one of his hairs was out of place, he'd have to run to the mirror to fix it.

Rowan stops to check his shoes. Becca passes him up and wins the unknown race to drop her paper in the finished work box. Emmanuel returns to his desk with his marked-up math paper in hand, and Becca plops down in front of me just as Rowan passes by, sticking his tongue out.

"Deal, Pinhead."

I don't have the usual regretful feeling of being paired with Bossy Becca. Instead, my stomach knots up like my bed tornado, and I want to bolt to the restroom.

Swallowing what feels like a lava rock, I deal the cards. No matter what, I need to let Becca win without giving away I'm doing it on purpose.

This is not going to be easy.

I deal the five cards out and turn the first number over for Becca to try and get. She picks it up in three cards. My turn gives me three cards too. Time to get started on the plan.

Becca takes her second turn and gathers only two cards. I turn over an odd number to make and immediately see I can gather all five cards. It takes all the self-control I can pull together to resist the urge to beat her. I really like to win. Trying to look the part of a kid who just doesn't understand math, I put my hand over my frowning mouth and proclaim, "Hm, I'm stumped."

The room is so quiet I can hear her bacon breath breathing in and out.

"Edison Taylor. What is the matter with you?" Becca tries to quiet her frustrated voice. "It's so obvious! I know you can see it as plain as the nose on my face. You can't fool me. You're up to something."

The RUBBER BAND

Busted.

Time to abandon the plan and just ask her to join the band.

"Okay, you got me." I take in a deep breath and exhale as fast as I can while speaking. "I'm wondering if you might be interested in being the lead singer in our garage band that we have entered in the Sun Valley Talent Show Contest."

Becca folds her arms and stares at me. Her steely eyes fix on mine. I can't back out now.

"Tell me more," she says as we pretend to play the game to avoid Miss Crenshaw separating us.

I lean in with a quick glance at Miss Crenshaw, and in my best playing the game pose, I whisper the deal to the one who could make or break the deal.

"Me and the guys started to practice in my garage last night, but we realized we needed a singer, or else we are just another boring instrumental rock band, and we want to be a REAL interesting rock band, the kind that brings people off their seats asking for more. I immediately thought of you punching it to 'The Star-Spangled Banner' and how amazing it was that morning before the flag salute."

Okay, this isn't the speech I'd practiced in my head, but it will have to do. I think I'm overwhelmed by her bacon breath or the glint of excitement I see in her eyes and forget my rehearsed speech. I notice a slight shift in how she sits, like instead of slumping over the cards, she straightens up. She must be thinking about what's in it for her. If she's considering it, I have to reel her in, so I go totally off my script again.

"You can come and check out the music we make after school. We're going to practice every day after homework for an hour and then longer on the weekends."

How can I make this worth her while? I don't have any bait, let alone a good hook to catch this fish and reel her in.

Why is she unusually quiet?

"Come on, Becca. Come check us out today. You know where I live, right?"

Silence.

"Last night my dad bought the band Joey's Pizza, and my mom made dessert. Who knows what goodies will come for us tonight?"

She unfolds her arms and pokes me in the chest with her pointer finger.

"I have a better idea. Why don't you bring the band to the Homecoming football game and watch me sing the National Anthem tomorrow night in front of hundreds of people, and then, MAYBE, I'll sing in your band."

I'd never been to a high school football game, so this could be fun. I'm sure the guys will go along with the deal. I can't wait until morning recess to tell them where we're going Friday night.

CHAPTER ELEVEN

Homecoming

The guys are excited about Friday night, not about hearing Becca sing, but because none of us have ever been to a high school football game. Dad makes all the arrangements with Roadkill's foster family, and Emmanuel's grandma got sick, so he can hang out with us all weekend.

I can tell Mom and Dad are thrilled to take us. They keep going down what they call "memory lane." Both of them graduated from Granite Hill High School, and they had gone to the Homecoming dance. As their story goes, they went with different dates but left the dance with each other. I've heard the story from them once or twice, and I feel relieved when they only mention it to my friends and don't go into details.

We arrive early to get choice seats in the bleachers. There isn't assigned seating, and I want to make sure I'm close enough to see how Becca performs without having to use the theater binoculars Dad brought. He says he likes to get a closer look at the players, but I figure he'll let me use them if I ask.

We settle three rows up from the bottom, so we can get a good view of the field. Roadkill sits with his hands stuffed in his jacket pockets. Next to Roadkill, Mom links her arm into Dad's and snuggles up to Dad's side. Oliver, Emmanuel, and I plop down in front of them.

The RUBBER BAND

The pep band plays as the teams run onto the field, taking sides to stretch and warm up. Raucous cheers roar from both sides of the crowd, but you can tell most of the people are rooting for the home team, Granite Hill, by how many of us cover our ears. If one of those noise-ometers was here measuring the volume, it would go all the way to the red zone and break.

All around us the colors of gold and blue create a flowing blanket of people cheering, screaming. The three of us get into the excitement when the cheerleaders line up in front of the bleachers and get the crowd to do the wave. I glance back to see Rocky up on his feet, hands in the air. For the first time, I see how straight his teeth are. His bright-white, toothy smile is wrinkling up his cheeks.

Inside, I cheer for him. It's good to see Rocky smile more.

"Ladies and gentlemen," the announcer breaks through the noisy crowd. I quickly turn my attention to the field and hope Rocky didn't catch me staring at him.

"Welcome to Granite Hill High School's Homecoming Game featuring our very own, growling grizzly bears!" As if on command, the crowd growls their best grizzly impression back at the announcer. I scan the field and sidelines, but there is no sign of Becca. The cold, metal bench chills my bum, and I squirm to keep warm.

"What's up with all the wiggling?" Oliver asks. "I'd say you're nervous. Do you like Becca or something?"

I stop wiggling.

"WHAT? NO! Never! EWWW ... Gross, just gross."

Truly, I am anxious, but there is no way in the world I would ever think of liking Becca. She had gotten me in trouble on purpose, and even though we desperately need her to be our lead singer, I'm not sure I can forgive her for smudging my perfect behavior record.

The announcer saves me from further humiliation.

"Granite Hill High School, let's welcome our royal court."

A giant, shiny white limousine pulls up in front of the grandstand, and the cheerleaders stand in a line on each side of the car's door, pom-poms held up high forming a fluffy canopy for the people inside to walk under. The driver comes around to open the door and holds out his hand to help step out in turn, three princesses in their fancy matching dresses. The pep band plays a processional march while the crowd cheers. The princesses' dates hand them each a bouquet of roses and walk them to a stage decorated like the throne room of a medieval palace. Their names and titles are announced as they take their seats to thundering applause, whistles, hoots, and cheers from the audience.

I scan the track for Becca, but in the sea of homecoming flashiness, she is nowhere to be found. I lose track of how many knots tie in my stomach, three or four or more, I think. I'm nervous about something. What if Becca says "no" to our offer?

The fanfare of trumpets takes my mind off my worries, and the crowd hushes. Everyone focuses on the limousine. Booming once again over the loudspeaker, the announcer croons, "Let's all congratulate this year's Homecoming queen …"

I don't pay attention to who the queen is because making her way onto the track is Bossy Becca herself, in a ruby red dress perched upon a white unicorn. Her long dark hair is braided into a bun on top of her head with tiny white flowers circling around it

Led by a woman dressed in riding clothes, they stop in front of the royal stage. With the queen on her throne, the announcer brings us to the moment we'd come for.

"And now, ladies and gentlemen, the royal court requests you stand for the National Anthem performed tonight by Miss Rebecca Chang of Wildwood Elementary School."

The RUBBER BAND

I reach back to Dad and ask for the binoculars to get a closer look. One of the royal guards helps Becca off the unicorn and up onto the stage. She has a wireless microphone taped to her cheek. I can see every rise and fall of her chest as she breathes. I can almost count the beads of sweat on her forehead. Is this what nervousness looks like? I remember my words from the other day about her choking the song and missing the notes. Nerves make a person do weird things, but I really want her to be awesome, and that means no squawking or warbling on the high notes.

The intro drum roll begins, and I hold my breath. I notice the knots again in my stomach as I swallow the lump in my throat. Becca stands straight and tall, takes a deep breath, and as the flag raises, her voice alone, acapella, breaks the silence.

"Oh, say can you see, by the dawn's early light."

I keep the lens on Becca's face. The melody flows effortlessly from her bright red lips—wait, is she wearing lipstick?

"What so proudly we hail, at the twilight's last gleaming."

Becca's eyes scan the crowd, looking for someone. Her face twinkles like a star, or is it the glittery makeup she wears—wait, is she wearing face makeup too? Whatever, it doesn't matter because at the moment, my heart races like it will break right out of my chest and fall beneath the cracks of the bleachers.

"Whose broad stripes and bright stars, through the perilous night, o'er the ramparts we watched, were so gallantly streaming." Her voice resonates through the stands, wafting up into the stars and beyond to the universe.

I know the next note is second to the hardest to hit. The knots in my belly pull tighter. Becca sucks in a massive breath and belts out in perfect pitch.

"And the rockets' red glare," the audience hoots and hollers as Becca holds out the note on the word glare. "The bombs bursting in air, gave proof through the night, that our flag was still there." She points to the now raised flag as background applause from the audience begins to rumble. Becca pauses, drops her hands to her sides, and takes another big breath slowing with each word.

"Oh, say does that star-spangled banner still wave."

This is the big finale. I'd heard Becca hit that high, final note in class. The note I had heard many professional singers struggle with as they sang before millions of people for a game on TV. Can Becca hit the note under all this pressure? Since I'm holding the binoculars, I can't cross my fingers for her to succeed, so I cross my ankles instead.

"O'er the land of the free." Her eyes close, and I spy a single tear dribbling from her eye as she holds out the note perfectly to the evening sky.

Bossy Becca has emotions!

I want to yell, "GO BECCA!" Thank goodness the audience's whistles and hoots take over instead but hush quickly for the split-second pause before the final line. Right then, Becca stares straight at me and holds my gaze until the end, slowing dramatically with each word.

"And the home of the brave!"

She pulls off the ending better than those TV performers, as the last note rings out to rumbling applause and cheers. And just like that, the performance is over. But not for me. I don't move or clap or anything. The binoculars stick to my face. A hard yank on my arm from Oliver, and I almost drop them.

"You can sit down now. The game's about to start." He shouts with a big grin. "Yep, it's gross alright."

I ignore my younger-by-two-minutes brother but keep watching Becca.

"That was Rebecca Chang, a third grader from Wildwood Elementary. She's going to be one to watch. Lookout

The RUBBER BAND

Hollywood, here she comes!" The announcer gives her credit once more as she waves and blows kisses to the crowd, absorbing all the cheers and attention of the spotlight. She curtseys to the royalty behind her and is helped off the stage by the woman handling the unicorn. The woman lifts her back into the saddle and leads her off the track out of sight.

"Did you hear what he said? Becca won't be able to stop telling everyone in class on Monday. She'll tell the whole school before morning recess." Oliver has a point. Becca loves to talk about herself.

"That was over-the-top brilliant!" Emmanuel yells over the noise from the crowd. "I can't wait to hear her do some rock 'n' roll with us."

I look back at Roadkill. He gives me a thumbs up. I guess that's his wordless way of saying Becca is a good choice.

"Well, she might like to talk about herself, but if she sings for us, she will also talk about the band, and that's free publicity, right?" I know things aren't going to be easy, but I have to put a positive twist on the situation. I keep scanning for Becca. She needs to come to practice tomorrow, especially since the guys approve.

I give the binoculars back to Dad. With the announcer going over the beginning lineup, I excuse myself saying I need to use the restroom, but really, I'm on a quest to see where Becca has gone.

Once behind the bleachers out of the view of the guys, I search for the color of bright red among all the blue. Where is she? I check the refreshment stand and the drinking water fountain. I stop to use the bathroom. Coming out, shaking the water from my washed hands, I notice a table against the back of the grandstand with a banner reading, "Special Guests." Behind it stands a photo booth with the lady and her unicorn, and a line of kids and adults waiting for a turn. My stomach knots up again. Becca stands next to the fake unicorn, getting her photo taken. I wait just beyond the table until she is finished.

"Great job, Becca." Do I put out my hand to shake hers as she approaches? Isn't that what a person does when congratulating someone? I lift my hand, but it's still dripping from washing, so I quickly wipe it on my jeans.

"Glad to see you came to hear me, Pinhead."

Did I have a choice in the matter?

"The crowd loved you. What I mean is, they loved you singing our National Anthem." I kick a pebble under the table, or was it a hardened wad of bubble gum? I really can't tell because I'm worrying about what to say next.

"Yes, of course they loved me. All the cheers and applause. I didn't want it to end." Her voice giggles. Her "all about me" attitude is clearer to me than a teenager's pimple-free face.

"Do you like my dress?" Becca spins around making her skirt flare out. A few of the tiny white flowers from her hair fall to the ground.

For a moment, I feel like my dad does when Mom asks him "How do I look?" I'm not sure what to say, and I certainly didn't come looking for Becca to tell her how pretty she looks. I just need to tell her what time to be at my house since we, the band, had completed her demand.

Before any awkward words can fall from my mouth, a couple pass by with a "You have a marvelous voice! Great job on the Anthem" followed by a man pointing a recorder in her face.

"Miss Chang, may I have a few words for the Sun Valley Times?"

I back away a couple feet to observe Becca getting more attention from the reporter. This is really going to increase the size of her already big head. If the newspaper mentions her name in a story or, worse yet, publishes a picture, her bragging will never end.

The RUBBER BAND

The interview lasts no more than five minutes, but I worry the guys will come looking for me. I'd been gone longer than the normal bathroom break, and if Oliver sees me with Becca, he'll for sure think I like her.

I need just a few more seconds with Becca to tell her what time to show up for practice, so as soon as the newspaper man left, I rush back.

"I think I'm going to be in the paper! Isn't that exciting? I can't wait to tell my parents! They'll be so proud of me. Maybe they'll buy me my own unicorn." Becca's words pour out faster than my mom's first cup of coffee in the morning. I just need a few words, and I'll be on my way.

"Becca, the band guys and I came to see you sing, and you really nailed it, perfectly."

"I know. I was better than perfect. I was phenomenal. I was heavenly. I was absolutely, positively, STELLAR."

My request is going to be challenging, especially since her head is in the clouds.

"Becca, Becca." I put my hands on her arms to stop her talking and hopefully pull her back down to earth. "Now, you have to complete your end of the bargain and come sing with us, in my garage, tomorrow."

Well, that worked. Becca's shoulders slump as I back off.

"Deal's a deal." She frowns. "What time?"

"About ten in the morning?"

She folds her arms, still frowning.

"I'm sure my mom will bake something yummy for brunch." Food bribing always works when it comes to convincing me.

The sides of her lips curl up into an almost smile.

"Does she make cinnamon rolls?"

Before I can answer, a man I've never seen before calls out.

"Miss Rebecca, it's time to go home now."

"Who's that?"

Becca sighs. "Albert, my driver."

Becca follows Albert, stopping as people give her pats on the back and handshakes. One little girl grabs her in a tight hug. I walk slowly behind until I reach the gate, and they go on to a fancy, expensive black car. Albert opens the back door, and Becca hops in. She rolls down the window and hollers back at me.

"See you tomorrow, Pinhead."

As the car drives off, I wonder where Becca's parents are.

CHAPTER TWELVE

Treasures

What will I tell the guys why I took so long to use the restroom? I've been gone longer than my dad when he's reading a magazine in the bathroom. I'll be in for some harassment from Oliver and Emmanuel for sure. Rocky won't care. He seems to be occupied with having a good time and won't have missed me at all. Still, I'll have to come up with a story to convince the guys I've been doing something other than talking with Becca.

My feet drag in the worn-down grass as I pass the welcome table on my way back to the grandstand. Then I spy it. Something shines from under the support beams of the bleachers. Little kids run around unsupervised down there as their parents watch the game above. With stealthy precision, I sneak under the grandstand and lay my hands on a silver dollar coin. I brush some mud off the back of the coin and stuff it in my pocket.

Wait one second.

I spy more coins scattered through the weeds growing over and around the support bars. Like a hungry wolf snuffing out a mouse in prairie grass, I scoop up everything that looks like a coin. Under the bleachers is a goldmine of change lost from unsuspecting adult pockets. In a few scavenging moments, I have my excuse for taking so long to get back and some really cool bottle caps to share.

The RUBBER BAND

The football game is halfway through the first quarter when I trudge up the steps back to my seat.

"Did you get lost, Eddie? You missed the kickoff and some helmet-smacking tackles." Oliver smirks. I can't outsmart him. He knows I'd been talking to Becca.

"Nope, just got a little sidetracked treasure hunting under the bleachers." Unfolding my fist, I show them the fruit of my alibi that amounts to $1.52 and three slightly rusty bottle caps. Emmanuel picks up the silver dollar as Oliver pokes at the rest of my stash.

"I'm sure there's much more to be had down there, but I didn't want you to get worried if I was gone too long." No one suspects at this point, and I thank my lucky charms, or whatever the saying is, I've avoided my brother's teasing.

"Eddie, we need to come back when no one is here and explore the whole place. My dad has one of those metal detector things, and I bet we could find a whole mess of cool stuff," Emmanuel shouts at me over the cheers of the crowd. Something good must have happened.

Rocky leans in from above us and picks up one of the bottle caps. He smirks, looks the treasured piece over a couple of times, shoves it into his pocket, and returns to watching the game.

I shrug, stuff my findings back in my pocket, and try to focus on the football field, but my mind wanders to Becca.

Wait a minute, she called the man her "driver?" I've never seen her parents drop her off at school in the morning, and since I usually come earlier than most kids, I never really pay attention. She'll just come wandering onto the playground, and I ignore her at all costs.

Why does she have a driver?

At halftime, the marching band comes onto the field wearing uniforms looking like tin soldiers with high hats and fluffy feathers. Instead of just playing in straight lines, they make patterns like stars and flowers and end with the shape of a bear to the cheering growls of the audience, all while making music. All of us boys, even Roadkill, join the crowd making bear growls. What kid can resist making weird noises?

The grizzly bear calls open a new realm of fun for us boys. We growl at everything that happens on the field whether it's good or not. We don't care. We clap, hoot, stomp our feet, and make every noise possible, even a few armpit farts. The situation is a veritable body-noise fest, and from the smell of things, I think we get away with more noises from our bodies than we care to admit.

At the blast of the two-minute warning, the score is seventeen to thirteen, in favor of the visitors. The game isn't looking good for the home team. But if I know anything from watching a couple of Super Bowl games, anything can happen in the last two minutes.

By this time, Granite Hill fans are on their feet making the noise-ometer arrow, if they had a noise-ometer, go way past the end and break the glass. They want to win pretty bad. The Grizzly Bears line up on the thirty-yard line, waiting for the snap. I pull out the binoculars hoping to read the lips of the quarterback, but he is talking too fast for me, and I don't know how to read lips anyway.

The play happens quicker than a cheetah chasing his dinner on the Serengeti. Granite Hill Grizzlies fake out the other team. Instead of passing the ball, they run in for a touchdown. The players pile on top of number eighty-eight in the end zone, crashing helmets. The fans go wild, breaking a third imaginary noise-ometer.

Kicking an extra point cinches the victory. Although, the other team makes a good show by lining up to attempt a comeback in the few remaining seconds. Unfortunately, seconds fly faster on the two-minute clock when your team is winning, and there aren't enough seconds left for the visitors to make a miracle.

Victory cannons shoot out gold and blue confetti raining down on us like a blizzard. I can't see the players on the field as they line up to shake hands. Confetti flutters around us, piling at our feet. I know instantly what comes next—

CONFETTI FIGHT!

Oliver grabs a handful from the bench and stuffs the confetti down Emmanuel's shirt. I toss a handful in the air, grab some more, and throw a wad at Emmanuel. I glance back at Mom and Dad who are celebrating their high school's win with a kiss.

EWWW! Gross!

Then something hits me. A big ball of blue and gold paper, smack dab in the side of my head. The paper wad came from none other than the kid I fear to challenge, Roadkill. A half-smirk grin crosses his face like he dares me to challenge.

In a moment of pure insanity, I whip a wad of shredded tissue paper back.

Bullseye!

Direct hit to Roadkill's nose.

I'm dead.

Ducking my head into my arm, I wait my doom. It doesn't come quick enough, so I dare to peek. Rocky's frown and squinty-eye stare blazes through me like a lightning bolt.

I really am going to die.

But, the most unexpected, unusual thing happens. Roadkill breaks into side-busting laughter.

My protecting arms drop to my sides, and I hiccup a nervous giggle turning into snorting fits of funny bone hoots, but not before I can wad up another ball of confetti and smack another one at him.

The scene becomes four boys stuffing tissue paper strips down every open pocket, hoodie, shirt, and loose waistband, having the time of their lives while surrounded by celebrating fans and mushy parents.

The night can't get any better.

"Hey, guys, we'd better get going. I promised I'd have you home at a decent hour, and we have a stop to make."

I know Dad is talking about our favorite ice cream shop, Close Cow Creamery or the triple "C" the locals call it. He almost always takes us there after movies or other events we go to. I'm already drooling over my order of a double scoop of bubble gum, cotton candy topped with mini marshmallows, chocolate sprinkles, and just to celebrate, gummy bears in honor of the Grizzly Bear win. This luscious concoction will fill my favorite syrup-flavored waffle cone, bringing a sugar coma to a diabetic should this concoction be eaten by one, but I never worry about that.

Leaving the paper-strewn football field, we follow my mushy, hand-holding parents to the van, picking paper pieces from our hair, ears, pockets, and other unmentionable places. Mom says she'd hate to be the one to clean up the mess. We boys are just happy to have been a part of making the mess.

Triple C has a long line of customers, but worth the wait. Rocky peruses the freezer case stretching the length of the shop. It's hard to make a choice with gallons of every flavor you can imagine in front of you, begging to taste them.

The kid behind the counter takes my order. I watch him filling my waffle cone with sugary goodness and notice Rocky, stuck in one spot, tapping his fingers on the protective glass over the ice cream options.

"Too many to choose from?"

The RUBBER BAND

Roadkill runs a hand through his thick hair and sighs. "They all look so good."

"You know, you can ask for a taste to help you decide. That's what the doll-size spoons are for. Just ask, and they'll dig a little out for you." The kid hands me my order, and I lick a gummy bear off before it can drop to the floor.

"My friend Rocky would like a sample. Go ahead, tell him what flavor you want to try." I know how hard it is to pick a flavor and then decide you want something else.

"Let's start with the first three in the front row." He directs the kid who follows Roadkill's request without skipping a beat. Roadkill licks the sample off each of the tiny spoons as if he's a judge at the fair.

"What's it going to be?" the kid asks.

"I'll try the next three flavors, and let you know." Roadkill stuffs the little plastic spoons in his jacket pocket. The kid hands him the next three samples, and once again, Roadkill licks each spoon in turn, then stuffs them in his pocket.

"You know, we have a bucket up here for you to put the dirty spoons in," the kid says. I'm sure he doesn't realize he's talking to Rocky Roadkill Espinosa because the kid taps his impatient fingers on the counter. His words and actions don't seem to faze Roadkill at all. Roadkill continues asking for samples, stuffing the spoons in his pocket until he has tasted every flavor of ice cream in Triple C's shop, despite the line of customers behind him. He clearly had a mission to complete. He stuffs his hand in his pocket and announces, "I'll have two scoops of vanilla with caramel and hot fudge in a cup."

Emmanuel, Oliver, and I snicker. I know the kid behind the counter can't say anything to Roadkill, but secretly, I wish he would, just to see Roadkill's reaction.

With our orders taken to-go, we all pile in the van again.

"Next stop, the Taylor house," Dad slurps a drip from his soft serve cone.

I think we all get brain freeze from swallowing our ice cream too fast.

"Surprise! The band is having a sleepover party!" Dad shouts.

"Yay!" Mom claps and cheers.

I'm excited, but my brain freeze hasn't thawed out. Oliver turns around with a spoon sticking out of his mouth. Emmanuel has a drip of chocolate syrup on his chin, but both have a look of terror in their eyes. Sitting next to me, Roadkill is stuffing his sundae, scoop by scoop into his mouth like it's the last ice cream he will ever have.

I know what Emmanuel and Oliver are thinking. Will we survive the night sleeping in the same room with Roadkill? I, for one, am up for the challenge.

We arrive home a couple hours past normal bedtime. Sleeping bags and pillows are already laying on the living room floor, and Mom sets out drinks and snacks.

"I know you guys are going to watch TV, play video games, and do weird boy stuff, but don't stay up late." Mom pours a bag of chips into a bowl. "You need to get rest for tomorrow's big band day."

"Don't worry, Mom." Oliver grabs a handful of chips. "I'm sure we'll survive no matter what."

"Okay then. Have fun." Mom winks at me and turns to go upstairs when Roadkill calls to her.

"Thank you, Mrs. Taylor."

"You're always welcome, Rocky."

Once Mom is out of sight, Oliver grabs the game controller. Emmanuel challenges him, and they are off to the

The RUBBER BAND

races with a go-kart game. Roadkill fluffs his pillow, spreads out a sleeping bag on the couch, taking the best spot for sleeping. I don't care. At least he's in a spot where we can keep an eye on him all night in case he tries to pull any pranks.

My dad thinks of everything when he plans stuff like this overnight. Both Roadkill and Emmanuel have a bag of their things waiting for them. I can't wait to get comfortable, so I run up to our room to put my PJs on. As I pull off my shirt, a fluff of gold and blue soggy confetti falls to the floor. I pick up the wad and go to the bathroom to throw it away. My back starts itching in a spot just out of my hand's reach. The kind of itch that contorts your body into a pretzel, and you still can't reach to scratch.

As I wriggle and twist in the battle to beat the itch, I spot something weird in the bathroom mirror. Blue and yellow spots appear on my back like the moldy cheese forgotten in the fridge. I almost freak out but remember all the confetti stuffed down my shirt at the game and how it probably stuck to my stinky, sweaty back, leaving blue and yellow color to paint my skin.

"Cool."

I have a temporary tattoo to show off to the guys. I bound down the stairs wearing just my pajama bottoms. Roadkill is opening a can of soda, and the other two are still racing on the TV screen.

"Guys, want to see something totally out of this world? I got a random tattoo!" My crazy announcement stops all activity. I proudly turn my back to the gang and show off the stains.

WHAM!

I'm struck by a soft projectile, knocking me sideways. I pick up the pillow, try to figure out who threw at me but get hit from behind. Oliver has declared war. Roadkill grabs his pillow from the couch, Emmanuel picks up his, and we pulverize each other with anything full of stuffing, including Mom's decorator pillows from that expensive designer store.

CHAPTER THIRTEEN

REHEARSAL–DAY 1

I wake up as the clock chimes three. After the pillow fight, video-game racing challenges, microwave popcorn, and one ridiculously long ghost story in the dark with flashlights under our chins for effect, the guys are sleeping soundly.

Moonlight shines through the window illuminating Roadkill on the couch. His hand hangs off the edge while the rest of his body disappears into the sleeping bag. The right side of his face smushes into the pillow, and a slime line of drool hangs from his mouth making a puddle.

In that moonlit moment, I realize something has changed in me.

Somehow, my fear of Roadkill flattening me for any reason he chooses no longer exists. I'm not sure when the fear left, but the lack of it makes me see a side of Roadkill not many kids notice. He lies there looking peaceful, maybe even happy, despite the drool bomb. If he has a mean-bone in his body, it's only because the kids at school spread a cruel rumor and gave him the nickname to match.

Although, Roadkill is a great name for a rock 'n' roll band drummer to have, he deserves some respect. From now on, I'm going to call him Rocky.

I fluff my pillow, turn over, and fall to sleep.

The RUBBER BAND

Waking up, the smell of cinnamon rolls baking wafts up my nostrils. Seeing the empty couch makes me think I had dreamed the whole sleepover thing, but I locate Rocky in the kitchen, helping Mom set the breakfast nook table. His sleeping bag has already been rolled, and the pillow lies on top neatly against the wall. Oliver wiggles in his sleeping bag, and Emmanuel is trying to beat his highest score on the video game.

The grandfather clock chimes nine. I've slept late, and panic tries to steal my hunger pains, trading them for butterflies. I wanted more time to feel ready before Becca arrived. There's a lot to do, but first, breakfast.

We don't say much at breakfast, mostly because we stuff the eggs, bacon, and cinnamon rolls down our throats with gulps of orange juice like we haven't eaten in months. Oliver and Emmanuel follow me to the garage. Rocky hangs back to help clear the table, but I overhear Mom insist he join us.

"Hey, guys." Emmanuel gathers us together. "Did anyone come up with some songs for us to try?"

Four guys with at least three tunes each make for a problem this little huddle didn't have time to solve. Becca will be here any minute, and anything can happen the minute she sets foot in the garage. The only thing we can agree upon is the song has to be something the crowd will recognize.

A car pulls into the driveway, and we stop talking. The garage is so quiet, I think I hear the mousetrap under the washing machine snap. We clamor to the side door to get a stealthy look.

Albert opens the door, helping Becca step out as Dad meets them.

Eavesdropping is the best way to get information. Not one of us makes a sound as we peer out the window, hoping not to be seen. Fortunately, Dad and Becca's driver speak loud enough for us to hear.

"I'm Albert, Miss Rebecca's caretaker."

I thought Becca said Albert is her driver?

"Nice to meet you. I'm Fred Taylor, Edison and Oliver's dad. Would you like to come in for some coffee and fresh cinnamon rolls while they practice?"

"That's mighty nice of you. Don't mind if I do. But first I should get Miss Rebecca's things and help her set up." Albert retrieves a hard case piece of luggage and a backpack from the trunk.

"Let me help you." Dad takes the backpack and leads Albert and Becca to the house walking past the garage window and our gawking eyes. We jump back into the garden rakes, sending them crashing against Dad's tool table. This, in turn, bumps a can of screws sitting on the table, scattering them to the floor. So much for trying to be stealthy. Our stakeout has been blown by our clumsiness.

We try to put them all back before Becca comes in but give up, scrambling to our feet as they walk in from the house entrance. We stand, frozen like ice sculptures. I swallow hard. I can't say for sure, but I think all four of us boys stop breathing in fear as Becca enters the room.

"Well, guys, are you ready for this or not?"

Visions of the dragon head from my nightmare come to mind as Becca struts to the middle of the garage and stops. With folded arms, she taps her left foot on the cement floor and scans the rafters and storage areas.

"Hmph," she groans. "It's not acoustically sound, but at such short notice, it will have to do. I'll work that out later. Albert, set up my music system."

Bossy Becca asked without even saying please.

The RUBBER BAND

Albert opens the travel bag and takes out what looks like a karaoke machine complete with a microphone and prompting screen. Dad helps him find an outlet and connect all the devices to the proper cords.

Becca stretches her arms to the rafters and then to the floor as if she were warming up for a race. Then she blows raspberries with her lips followed by odd sentences sounding like things you'd say to make a baby laugh. We guys watch unmoving, stunned by her actions.

Becca stops in the middle of bending in half, stretching her arms out like an airplane, and lifts her head slightly to meet our baffled stares.

"Are you guys going to warm up or what?"

Rocky goes straight to the drum set, pulling out his sticks. Oliver takes to the keyboard while Emmanuel straps on his bass. We play random notes and rhythms on our instruments like we know what we are doing as Albert and Dad finish plugging things in and go into the house.

As the door closes, my fingers stop stroking the guitar strings.

This is the moment of truth. A time of reckoning. Do or die.

Seeing Becca in my sawdust sprinkled, spiderweb-ridden, mouse-infested garage meant facing the dragon, conquering my fear, and getting on with the dream of winning the Sun Valley Talent Show Contest.

Here goes nothing.

"Listen up." My voice goes unnoticed.

Maybe I'll just start playing.

Closing my eyes, I strum a note, quavering like a rock star on his knees doing a solo before a few thousand fans. The crowd chants my name, going wild as I crawl across stage continuing the rift. The sound echoes into the great unknown, then falls quiet.

I open my eyes.

Becca, Oliver, and Emmanuel stand over me, bewildered looks on their faces. I let my daydreaming get out of hand.

"Are you finished, Pinhead?" Becca blurts as I scramble to get up without dropping my guitar.

"Yep, I'm just warming up." I brush sawdust off my arms.

"I've got a ballet lesson, so I can only be here until noon." Becca picks up the microphone and scrolls through the karaoke screen. "I have thousands of tunes on this thing."

"We've already chosen some songs." I try to take charge, but Bossy Becca interrupts.

"Like I said, I've got them all. Give me a title, and I'll pull it up."

"I can get my dad to print out our choices, so we have music to follow."

Becca's hands go to her hips as she shakes her head.

"We don't need sheet music. Just listen and play along."

"I like the sound of that." Rocky's voice stops my frustration before it can get the best of me.

I don't want Becca to take charge. This is my garage, my idea, and my band.

"Eddie, let's give it a try. We can barely read music anyway. Besides, not printing out the music will save some trees." Emmanuel has what Dad calls "a good head on his shoulders."

"Yeah, Eddieeee …" Oliver always holds out the last vowel on my name when he is up to something. The mischievous look on his face tells me he is going to humiliate me. His words from the football game last night about Becca slam into my thoughts. For a minute, I am tempted to deck him, but fortunately for him, I lapse into self-control, and let it go.

The RUBBER BAND

"Okay, but we don't want to do anything slow. It has to be fun, fast, and rock 'n' roll the audience will recognize." At least I can give her rules to follow.

"How about this one?" Becca presses play, and the music to "I Love Rock 'n' Roll" rings out of the karaoke amplifier. Becca puts the microphone to her mouth and sings the lyrics off the screen in front of her.

Rocky picks up his sticks and joins the beat while the rest of us just listen. Becca crunches the words with a raspy sound like her throat is sore. The words make us giggle. The song is all about a girl checking out a guy at the jukebox, wanting to dance with him. The song is definitely an oldy, and one the crowd would recognize.

Becca's voice sounds amazing, and she adds body movements while she sings like she's already on stage. Despite the embarrassing words, and our occasional snickers, along with Rocky's drumming, she nails it.

Oliver, Emmanuel, and I clap, whistle, and whoop like fans.

"Let's try another one." She swipes the tablet with a touch of her finger.

"Okay, but can we do something where the words aren't so, um ..." I stumble as my personal embarrassment thermometer goes past one hundred degrees, flushing my face, "... adult?"

"What's the matter, Pinhead. They're just words." Becca has the dragon-face look from my dream. I know we'll find the perfect tune to play. One that won't make me turn three hundred shades of red. The song we decide on just isn't going to be "I Love Rock 'n' Roll" from the 80's menu.

"I think we should look at everyone's ideas before we decide."

Becca's steely stare shoots through me like a cannonball, I feel like the live version of what you see in cartoons. Her stare leaves a gaping hole in my stomach so big I'm certain you can see right through me to the garage door. For a moment, I have second thoughts about inviting her to join us, but we decided not to be the boring band at the contest without a singer, and she is our only option to non-boring.

"Emmanuel," she points her dragon talon at him, "what should we do next?"

He shrugs. "Doesn't matter to me."

"Oliver?" Becca turns to my brother. He doesn't move.

"Born to be Wild." Rocky stands tall and confident behind his drums.

Becca types in the title. "I like it. Let's listen first, then the second time, I'll sing, and you guys can play along."

"Before we get started, I need to use the bathroom." True, I'm not trying to escape. I do need a break to catch my breath before I completely lose it and shoot a bagful of rubber bands at Becca. I'm also on the verge of doing the pee-pee dance.

The music plays as I slip into the hallway bathroom. Rocky's idea to try that song is a good one. If we can pull it off, maybe we'll stand a chance to win the contest. Of course, I really want to win. That's what this is all about.

Winning.

On my way back to the garage, I can hear Albert and Dad at the kitchen table enjoying coffee and Mom's cinnamon rolls. I creep close to hear what they are talking about.

"How long have you been Rebecca's caretaker?" Dad sips his coffee.

"I started with the Chang family a little over twelve years ago as a handyman assisting the housekeeping staff. But as time went on and Miss Rebecca was born, the Changs asked me to do more, and before I knew it, I was pretty much taking care of Miss Rebecca full time." Albert takes a bite of a cinnamon roll. "Mm, mm, this has to be the best roll I've ever tasted."

The RUBBER BAND

"Yes, my wife is an excellent baker, cook, artist. Anything she does is out-of-this-world, at least in my eyes."

Listening in on someone's private conversation makes me feel like a criminal, but I can't help myself. I'll take any information on Bossy Becca I can gather.

"If I may ask, what kind of work do Rebecca's parents do for a living?"

Albert shifts forward in his chair, taking a sip of his coffee. I can't wait to hear the answer, and nearly blow my cover as I hold back an annoying sneeze. Someone told me once I can stop a sneeze by thinking of grapefruit, so I give it a try.

Grapefruit. Grapefruit. Grapefruit.

To my surprise, it works.

"Mr. Chang is in the movie business and travels a lot. He's currently in Nepal working on a documentary for National Geographic."

"That sounds fascinating. Is Mrs. Chang with him?"

"No, unfortunately not. Most of the time their schedules take them far apart. It's not often they're home together."

Even though I want to stay and hear the entire conversation, I've been gone too long and need to get back to the band.

"Did everything come out all right?" Oliver's comment creates snickers from the guys and a devilish look from Becca.

I ignore them and strap on my guitar.

"AH, AH AHCHOOOO ..." The backed-up sneeze erupts like the volcano in Hawaii, blowing a stream of spit and boogers across the room.

"Ewww! That's disgusting." Becca's face wrinkles like a prune.

The guys practically roll on the floor, laughing.

"God bless you," Rocky adds.

"Thank you." My sneeze drippings have blown past my guitar, but my nose feels wet, so I wipe it on my sleeve.

Becca shakes her head. I don't think she hangs out with boys very often.

"Now, let's give that song a try." I strum the strings in the key of D.

My heart wants to play, but my mind hangs on what I'd overheard.

Becca's driver is her caretaker because her parents are never there for her. The idea made me think about how I acted the time Mom and Dad wouldn't let me jump off the high dive at the public swimming pool.

I might have overreacted.

They were just being good parents, taking care of me, and keeping me safe. I was only five and couldn't swim without water wings on my arms. I wonder if Becca's parents ever kept her from sinking in the deep end.

Becca pushes play and counts a beat. Her raspy rock 'n' roll voice hits the notes like a pro while the rest of us add sounds of music here and there building our confidence with each note. Everything starts to feel good as we pick up on the music cues, until out of nowhere, without warning, Becca screams.

CHAPTER FOURTEEN

CHOICES

Becca jumps on top of the washing machine. Her feet take turns lifting like they are cooking on a hot griddle. She isn't singing. She's screaming.

Dad and Albert throw open the door and rush in like firemen on a rescue.

"Miss Rebecca, are you all right?" Albert scoops her up. She wraps her legs around his body and her arms around his neck and squeezes so tight, his face almost turns blue. She looks like one of those baby monkeys, afraid to let go of its mother.

"M-M-Mouse!" Becca screeches.

I've seen mice run across the garage floor many times. I'm sure Becca's house doesn't have a pest problem. My guess is she has never seen a cobweb except the fake ones at Halloween.

"Sorry," Dad says. "We've been trying to catch that smart mouse for months. He usually only comes out at night."

Becca peeks from her near-death grip on Albert's neck and glares at us guys. We stare back without a word. I wonder if she is going to stay or if that pesky mouse has ruined everything for the band. We've just gotten started, and I can't let anything stop the dream from happening.

"It'll be okay, Miss Rebecca. That little guy is probably as scared of you as you are of him." Albert tries to loosen Becca's grip on his neck, but she pinches tighter.

The RUBBER BAND

"I'll get a stool from the house, so you can be higher up if the mouse decides to be brave and show up again." Dad's attempt to calm Becca works a little as she loosens her arms and faces Albert.

"You're not going to be far away, are you, Albert?"

Now this is a side of Bossy Becca I've never seen before. Meekness is not a dragon trait.

"I can stay in here if you want me to. Otherwise, I'll be right inside the door, ready in a split second if you need me."

Becca focuses on Albert's gaze and then rubs her hand over the stubby grey hairs of his balding head. She kisses his cheek, whispers something in his ear as he sets her down.

"Now, where were we before we were so rudely interrupted?" Becca takes a familiar stance with her hands on her hips.

Dad brings the stool for Becca, and soon it's just the band again. The music rolls out of the speakers, and we join in, plodding along as best we can. Rocky picks up the beat quickly. Emmanuel's fingers pluck a few bass notes while Oliver tries his best to tickle the piano keys. Me, well let's just say, I'm not so good at playing by ear. The notes I attempt are offbeat and off-key. Anything I play sounds so terrible, even the resident mouse might need ear plugs.

Once through the song, Becca seems to forget about the mouse situation and slips off the stool. "It's going to need some work, but I think we have the song for the contest." She's taking charge again.

Wait one second. Who does she think she is telling us what we are going to play? My pulse quickens. The veins on my neck always pop out when I get upset. I stroke my neck to check. Yep, they bulge out like a muffin top. Time to put a stop to Becca's control.

"I think we should take a vote." Words pop out of my mouth before my racing heart can stop them. I have to let her know this is MY garage, MY idea, MY BAND!

Rocky gives me a thumb's up. Oliver's grin spreads across his face like peanut butter on bread.

"Great idea, Eddie. Let's vote. Raise your hand if you want to play 'Born to be Wild' in the contest." I'm happy Emmanuel's level head takes over because my knees are wobbly in fear of getting devoured by a dragon.

The vote is unanimous. All five agree.

"Okay, let's get started, I'm running out of time." Becca pushes play, and we fumble our way through again, not sounding any better than the first time we tried, except for Becca. A little voice inside my head tells me her golden-buzzer voice will win the contest for us.

There isn't a clock in the garage, so we have no idea what time it is until Albert comes in announcing it's time to pack up Miss Rebecca for her ballet lesson. He suggests leaving the equipment since Miss Rebecca will be coming back every day after school to rehearse.

I can't get over Albert always calling her Miss Rebecca like she deserves his respect or something.

Before Becca leaves, we set a time to meet after school each day until the contest. We don't have a lot of time on the calendar to prepare, but at least, we've gotten closer to the goal by agreeing on a song and setting up practice times.

"We picked the right tune." Rocky stuffs his drumsticks in their usual spot, his jean back pocket.

Everyone stops moving. To our amazement, Rocky spoke.

"You got that right, Road-um, Rocky." For a moment, I'd forgotten my new respect for our drummer.

"Think about it, Pin—I mean Eddie." His smile creases his cheeks with mischief. Even Becca looks surprised

The RUBBER BAND

I try to think, but fear gets the best of me, and I can't speak. I may have new respect for Road-I mean Rocky, but he's still scary.

"Dude. It's as obvious as Mr. Haymaker's bald head." Rocky isn't giving this one up, and even though I try, no words will come from my mouth.

"Mr. Haymaker's bald head! That's a good one Rocky." Emmanuel fist-bumps Rocky without a second thought.

"Don't we go to WILDwood Elementary School?" Rocky's voice emphasizes one syllable in particular.

"Yeah, so what?" Then like the morning sunrise, the emphasized syllable dawns on me. I'm so focused on my ideas for the band, the thought didn't occur to me how perfect our choice of song is.

Chuckles cluck from deep within me joined by snickers and laughs from the band.

"Okay, I get it. The band from Wildwood Elementary playing 'Born to be Wild' sounds like a winner to me."

With Becca gone, the guys can't wait to get their hands on the karaoke machine.

"She wasn't kidding about how many tunes this thing has." Oliver runs his finger over the selections.

"This is so cool. The words go across the screen along with the music." Emmanuel points to a selection. "If you get lost, just follow the star that bops in time across the lyrics."

"Let's try it out." Oliver keeps searching.

"Wait a second. Hold up guys. I don't think Becca will like us messing with her equipment like this." I try to stop them, but Oliver makes a choice, grabs the microphone, and taps his foot to a beat, ready to sing along.

A Beatles' tune we know from music class at school comes through the speaker. When the chorus starts, we join Oliver, singing ridiculously loud, "We all live in a …"

Like an avalanche, the music snowballs and rolls on nonstop. We can't help but line up our favorite songs and take turns belting them out, on-key or not. Even Rocky picks up the microphone to imitate Elvis's "Hound Dog."

At one point, all our fingers are on the screen fighting to choose. Laughter roars freely, and comments pour out on who we think should sing what song, filling the garage with happy sounds. We scroll through the choices, picking ones that fit our individual personalities, and challenging each other to belt out a tune. If it weren't for Mom calling us to come have a snack, we'd have done karaoke all day.

Monday morning, the entire school buzzes over Sunday's front-page newspaper article about the Homecoming win with a huge picture of Becca singing the National Anthem, striking a patriotic pose.

Miss Crenshaw makes a big deal about the article as she reads it to the class. When she's done reading, Becca shares her version of the story before we do the pledge. As I listen to the real happenings get blown up to proportions of enormous, unmeasurable size, Saturday's mouse event comes back to my mind. Yeah, Becca likes to talk about herself and control everything, but one little mouse can turn her cement wall into Lego bricks.

Our predictions are correct. I giggle about Becca's head being puffed-up over the big news story. It talks details about the game and only mentions her name in a caption under the photo.

The RUBBER BAND

"Do you have something to say, Edison?" Miss Crenshaw doesn't miss anything.

My face burns raging hot red, like I suddenly need an air conditioner to cool down my embarrassment.

"Nope."

"Then please continue, Rebecca."

Oliver snickers, and Emmanuel shakes his head. We know the truth. All it takes is one garage mouse to bring Bossy Becca back to earth.

At lunch recess, Emmanuel, Oliver, and I sit at our usual table. Pulling out my peanut butter sandwich, I chomp a huge bite, showing off the U-shaped teeth marks as Rocky plops down next to me. I nearly choke on a gob of peanut butter. Rocky chomps into a Christmas-red apple.

"What?" Rocky has a line of apple juice dribbling from the side of his mouth. He eyeballs each one of us in turn.

I take a swallow from my water bottle.

"Nothing." I smile. "Nothing at all."

But really, I know it is something. Roadkill Rocky is my friend, and now the entire school knows too.

CHAPTER FIFTEEN

2ND PRACTICE

"Hey, Eddie," Oliver mumbles from his side of the room. "You done with your homework yet?"

"I would be if you didn't keep asking me if I am done!"

As third graders, we don't get a lot of homework like they do in the upper grades, but the Taylor house rules are you have to finish your homework before you do anything else after school. I finish my math paper and begin working on spelling when I hear a car pull in the driveway.

"Hurry up and finish. Bossy Becca is here." Oliver tosses a wad of paper, missing my head and landing at my feet. "You don't want to keep your girlfriend waiting."

That comment crosses a line.

I can't get off my chair fast enough to pull Oliver down to the floor, decking him.

"If you don't knock it off, I'm going to pulverize you!" My fist balls up. Oliver winces.

"You like her. Admit it." His words give fuel to my anger.

I pull my fist back, ready to punch his smirking face. I've never hit Oliver in any of our squabbles, but he deserves it this time. My fist knocks him right in the nose, surprising me more than him. A trickle of blood drizzles from his left nostril.

Oliver's eyes fill with tears. My hand pulses in pain.

What have I done? I'm not a violent person. I'm the peacekeeper.

The RUBBER BAND

"I'm sorry, I'm sorry, I'm sorry." I can't say it enough.

Oliver wipes his nose with his hand. Seeing the blood, his eyes turn ice cold, a look I've never seen before. I back off, sitting at his side.

Staring at the floor, I can't bring my eyes to meet my twin's gaze, but I can feel his. I'd jousted him off his horse in the first round.

WHAP!

Oliver blindsides me with a pillow strike to the head, toppling me sideways.

Okay, so maybe he survives for the second round.

I grab the largest pillow I can find and retaliate with a giant wallop, knocking him facedown to the floor. We forget about finishing our homework and Bossy Becca's arrival, as we pulverize each other. We would've kept on fighting until the feather pillows broke open, but Mom appears at our door, arms folded.

Oliver doesn't say a word to Mom about the bloody nose. Instead, we make our way to the garage, in silence. I'm sure Mom knows something is up because moms are notoriously known for knowing everything. They have eyes in the back of their heads. I've never actually seen the eyes. Let's just say, I know they exist from experience.

"Oliver, what happened to your nose?" The back-of-the-head eyes are working after all, and I am in trouble.

"Eddie accidently hit me during our pillow fight," he takes a breath, "I'm fine, Mom."

"Let me take a look." She cups his chin in one hand and examines him with the other. "I'll bring you an ice pack to keep it from swelling. Worse case, you might get a black eye."

Oliver knows better than to argue with Mom. She leaves to find him an ice pack, and we go to the garage.

Becca is doing weird stretches again, making the goofy noises, and blowing raspberries. Why does Oliver think I like her?

"You're late!" Becca snaps.

"No, you're EARLY." Oliver snaps back, smearing a drop of blood off with his arm. Now, I really feel bad for punching him.

"You know what they say about early birds, right?" Becca's hands are on her hips, and she's tapping one foot. She poses like that so much she could get a job as a model in a sculpture studio. If she were tagged in a game of freeze tag, that's how she'd stand until someone unfroze her. I mean to say, IF someone unfroze her.

Mom pops in with an ice pack for Oliver. Becca raises an eyebrow but immediately goes back to taking control.

"And where is the drummer and bass player?"

Why doesn't she ask for them by name? The way she refers to Emmanuel and Rocky is like she doesn't know them at all. Wildwood is a small school. Everyone knows everybody by their first name.

I've had enough of her demands already, and we haven't played a note.

"The rules of our house and the agreement we made as a band are you must finish your homework before coming to practice."

"Well, my tutor already helped me finish my homework."

Becca has a tutor? I thought tutors were only needed if you were failing?

"The guys will be here. What's your hurry anyway? You got another ballet lesson to get to?" Today, I'll make every effort to keep her from bossing the band around.

The RUBBER BAND

As if on cue, Mom opens the door, letting Rocky and Emmanuel in. She checks on Oliver's nose and insists he keep the ice pack on for a few more minutes.

"I've set out some snacks for when you kids get hungry." Mom always takes care of important business first. "I'll be in the studio if you need anything."

Just like that, the band is alone, in awkward silence.

Becca continues stretching without the funny sounds. Emmanuel and I ready our guitars. Rocky hits the drums with a random beat, and Oliver joins him on the keyboard.

Since this is how we started out the other day, it must be how a band warms up, making random notes, pieces of music not attached to anything but our own thoughts.

I can get used to this.

SCREEEEECH!

An awful noise like fingernails across a chalkboard squawks from the karaoke speaker, stopping our random music.

Becca's face looks like a deer caught in headlights.

"Oops. I forgot about the reverb." She backs away from the speaker. "Now that I have your attention, let's get started."

Becca plays the tune through once while we listen for our individual parts. This might be harder than I thought. Becca took charge. Again.

"Now, you guys give it a try." Becca pushes the play button once more, and we struggle through the song. We sound like a symphony without a director. In one word, horrible, with a capital H.

When the song finishes, not one of us moves. I wait for the mousetrap to snap and wake us up. I'd also like to see Becca do her scream and dance routine on top of the washing machine again.

Second thoughts about the contest fill my brain to overload. What have I gotten us into?

"Do you guys want the good news or the bad news, or just the bad news because there doesn't seem to be any good news?" Becca's hands are on her hips again.

"What are you talking about?" Oliver asks. I'm sure Rocky and Emmanuel have the same question. I, however, know exactly what she's talking about.

"Is it too late to withdraw from the competition?"

"What?" The guys shout in protest, and Rocky stands, waving his drumsticks in the air. I don't say a word.

"You guys sound terrible," Becca shouts back. "You aren't playing together, and the music is all over the place. The only one that seems to keep up is Roadkill, and even he is struggling."

Now, it's one thing to insult my friends, but it's a whole other thing to call Rocky by his secret nickname from school. The garage got quiet. I glance at Rocky. He sits on his stool, arms crossed with a drumstick in each hand poking upward. He looks like a skull and crossbones with skin. His rolled-up T-shirt sleeves show off his bulging bicep muscles begging for a tattoo to complete his motorcycle gang look.

Becca crossed a line. We don't move in anticipation of what might happen next. From my vantage point, I can't see what the other guys are doing. I just stare at the cement floor following a crack to where it begins at the wall.

"You guys think I don't know what everyone calls me? I'm not deaf or blind. I know the entire school is afraid of me, the big bad bully. No one dares talk to me for fear I'll run them over, flatten them like a dead raccoon on the highway, or beat them with my drumsticks."

What do you do when faced with a sticky, uncomfortable situation? It isn't like we need an adult to fix it. This is something we can deal with ourselves. The crack in the floor loses its appeal to me. I try to calm the storm before it becomes an F5 tornado.

The RUBBER BAND

"Hey, Rocky. I'm sure Becca didn't mean anything."

"Yeah, Bossy Becca didn't mean anything." Oliver blurts his thoughts.

Becca crosses her arms and taps one foot, again.

"What did you call me?" The dragon wakes up, snarling.

"You heard me." Oliver is a safe distance from dragon breath behind his keyboard.

Someone has to do something before this name-calling session gets out of hand.

"Let's get back to playing music." I pluck a flat-sounding note on my guitar and adjust the tightness of my strings on the tuning pegs.

"There's not going to be music. I'm calling Albert right now to come and get me and my equipment. This gig is over, Pinhead." Becca pulls the cord from the karaoke machine before any of us can say a word, except for one brave drummer.

"You're going to run off just because you heard what kids call you? I can count on both hands how many times a day I hear 'Roadkill' whispered behind my back. You can dish it out, but you can't take it? How do you think Eddie feels about being called Pinhead?"

Becca stops moving.

Rocky points a drumstick at her. "You're afraid. That's why you call me and other kids names." Rocky takes a breath. "Tell me, who's the bully now?"

Just when I think the dream of the band is dead, the miracle of resurrection happens.

Becca plugs the cord back into the karaoke machine.

"I'm here for no other reason than to win this contest. It'll be nothing short of impressive on my singing résumé."

Nothing works better than changing the subject.

Just like that, we get back to playing.

We slog through the song a couple of times without one mention of the name-calling argument. Albert arrives on time to pick up Becca, and she leaves the karaoke equipment behind. I guess that means she'll be coming back tomorrow.

Chapter Sixteen

Karaoke

If the television weatherperson could register atmospheric pressure in a garage, the pressure is definitely higher than the roof. Becca's comments scratched opened some scabbed-over wounds. After she left, even the walls holding garden equipment and storage shelves relaxed.

With dragon-breath Becca gone, we heave one huge sigh and are breathing normal again. I've never called Becca names to her face. After Rocky's words, I'm starting to feel guilty even thinking of calling her a name besides Becca.

"Dudes, are we sure she's the right singer for this gig?" Emmanuel speaks the words we are all thinking.

Rocky ignores the comment and strolls over to the karaoke machine. His fingers scroll through the screen options.

"Hey, guys, let's give this thing a workout." He picks up the microphone and pushes play, belting out the words of another Beatles' tune.

If Becca knew what we were doing with her precious equipment, she'd throw a fit worse than when she saw the mouse. But that doesn't matter to us. We try songs we know and songs we don't, taking turns while the others pretend to be judges. Sometimes we join together on a chorus of an oldie everyone knows the words to.

Rocky uses his sticks to play imaginary drums, and soon we are all playing air instruments, jumping off the washing machine like we are stagediving into the audience. The garage our stadium, we play encore after encore until Mom shows up like security holding back fans trying to climb over the stage barriers.

"Okay, band, this roadie says practice time is over. Dad's ready to drive Rocky and Emmanuel home."

To my surprise, everyone groans.

"Really, Mom, already? We are just getting started." Oliver grumbles.

Before anyone can add more complaints, Rocky speaks.

"Okay, Mrs. Taylor. Thank you for having us," and he walks out the door with his drumsticks poking out of his back jeans pocket.

Tuesday morning, I finish the wake-up work Miss Crenshaw gives us first thing before lessons start to wake up our brains if we happen to still be sleepy. I sit on the floor and wait for a math games partner, thinking about how kids give each other nicknames. Nicknames can be fun. Sometimes the person loves the name, sometimes they don't. I've heard for some people a nickname sticks forever. Mom and Dad told us stories about longtime friends who still go by names they were tagged with going all the way back to elementary school.

My eyes look at Becca. She is taking an awfully long time getting done. She obviously doesn't like the nickname we all gave her. Unfortunately for Becca, she really is bossy. The alliteration of the letter Bs in Bossy Becca make sense, fitting her perfectly.

I suddenly feel the urge to run to the restroom, and Miss Crenshaw knows I am desperate because she waves me quickly to the door. Teachers have instincts about student bodily functions, so they don't always have to say directions out loud.

After the restroom, I take an extra-long drink. I can't believe how thirsty I am. As the water washes down my throat, I feel like I am watering the Sahara Desert. My thirst refuses to be quenched. I can drink cold water all day, but I have to stop slurping down water because an impatient first grader's nonstop pokes on my back force me to stop and let the shrimp take his turn.

Back at class, Becca is playing math games with another girl. As I walk past Miss Crenshaw, she points to the clock on the wall.

"Eddie, you were gone way too long for a bathroom break."

I didn't mean to take so long, and I've never been a "staller" when it comes to schoolwork. I'm just so thirsty. I'd still be drinking water if it hadn't been for that pesky little kid.

Halfway to recess, I have to go. Again.

Miss Crenshaw wrinkles her nose at my second request in less than an hour but allows me to leave. I stop for another drink to ease my unquenchable thirst but don't take as long this time to avoid trouble.

When the recess bell rings, I stop at the water fountain and take an extra-long drink, even when a line of fifth and sixth graders stand behind me. I don't care if I get pulverized, the Sahara thirst takes priority over my personal safety.

Emmanuel and Oliver are at our usual table outside as I sit down. The birds had been busy overnight as there are more bird droppings than usual all over the table.

My thirst drives me to my grape juice box, and I suck on the straw so hard, the box collapses in exhaustion.

"Where have you been?" Oliver knows I'd usually race to the table, scarf down my snack, and hit the basketball court as soon as possible.

The RUBBER BAND

Posing like an NBA player at the free throw line, I ignore Oliver and toss the empty box into the open trash can for the winning point.

"And the crowd goes wild!" I high five my tablemates just as Rocky sits next to me.

He raises his palm, joining in on my victory, and nothing stops me from a hand-smacking high five right back at him.

The guys must be getting used to the fact Rocky isn't as scary as he looks. They don't freeze up or get all sweaty-nervous in his presence. He joins us on the basketball court and wins the first round of dynamite ball.

Dynamite ball is a game we made up where the first person in line shoots, and if they make the shot, you have to make the same shot or you're out. If they don't make the shot, you have to get the rebound before the ball hits the concrete or you're out too. If you get the rebound, you get to choose where to take the next shot. This goes on until the last one wins. Sometimes we don't have enough time at morning recess, and we have to continue the game at lunch.

Rocky, being a fourth grader, has a height advantage over us third graders, which is probably why he wins this game. Or maybe we let him win because he is known for being a bully, and we're still afraid of what he might do to us.

Before the bell rings calling us back to class, I run to the drinking fountain. My dry mouth feels like I ate a full saltshaker.

Four o'clock on the dot, the band starts arriving in time for our Tuesday afternoon practice. Becca strolls in wearing a T-shirt sporting a large red mouth with its tongue hanging out. I've seen the mouth before. Some band from the 70s used it as a symbol because the lead singer had a big mouth.

"Let's get this show on the road." Becca picks up her microphone and turns on the karaoke machine. "I'm wearing my genuine Rolling Stone's T-shirt signed by Mick Jagger himself to help me focus."

"Who is Jagged Mick, and don't you have to warm up, do those funny stretches, and make weird noises first?" Oliver presses a sour-sounding note on his keyboard.

"Nope. I did some in the car on the way over. Mick JAGGER is a rock icon. My parents met him backstage when Daddy was filming a music video for him. This shirt is worth a ton of money." Becca pulls the shirt down at the hem, making the tongue stick out from her belly.

"Isn't this awesome? My favorite shirt of all time since it has Mick's germs all over it. I'll never let the housekeeper wash it."

"I'm wearing my favorite underwear, and I won't let my mom wash them either!" Oliver quips.

"And your germs are definitely all over them!" Emmanuel adds.

His humorous comment sends us boys into gut-snorting laughter.

Becca puts the microphone to her mouth, getting our attention.

"STOP! You guys are nothing short of disgusting! We can't waste time. I've got to get out of here fast today. My toes desperately need a pedicure, and I can't miss my five-fifteen appointment." She pauses, looks down at the karaoke machine, and frowns. "Wait a second. I left this machine set on 'Born to be Wild.' WHO CHANGED THE SETTING?"

Becca's words boom through the speaker so loud we clap our hands to our ears.

The dragon doesn't like anyone messing with her stuff.

"I left this here in good faith, and you guys touched it, didn't you!"

The RUBBER BAND

If we are going to get any practice done, someone has to do or say something fast because the dragon is about to spit fire and burn us to the ground.

"We're sorry, Rebecca. Aren't we, guys?" Rocky's humble voice is unusual, but it's the firehose we needed to put out the flame.

"We're sorry, Becca."

"Can we rock-out now?" Rocky asks, staring down the fury of a doused dragon.

"Fine." Becca taps a foot in time, counting out the start, as the rest of us scurry faster than our garage mouse to pick up and play our instruments.

Halfway through the song, I have to pee, but there is no way I can stop in the middle after how practice began. I start dancing about like a real rock star until the song ends, then whip off my guitar and run into the house, getting to the bathroom just in time.

On the way back, I stop at the fridge for some bottled water, gathering up one for each of the band and an extra for my unquenchable thirst.

"Eddie, are you all right? You raced in here like you were running from a fire." Mom doesn't miss a thing.

"Just had to take a quick break and bring refreshments." There's no time to talk with Mom. Becca needs to get to her "cure" thing, and I don't want to make her angry again.

The ice-cold water bottle peace offering helps to smooth things over.

Becca takes the water gratefully, and after a couple of swigs each, we get back to the music, except for me. I guzzle both bottles so quick, I give myself hiccups.

My hiccups don't stop Becca from pushing play since I don't have to sing. I hold my breath, hoping the hiccups will go away. I get so involved in the music, my hiccups disappear somewhere between the first mention of the lyric "wild" and the second verse.

Dad comes in to hear the last few bars and claps. "Sounds like you're ready for me to film your audition video."

"Can't we wait another day, Mr. Taylor? We don't sound too great." Becca's knee is jerking, and her face looks like she saw the mouse again.

"They don't need your audition to be perfect. You guys sound great already, and I think whoever does the choosing will be impressed with a kid band that plays oldies. We have to get the video in before the deadline, and I think you're ready, only you'll have to do without the karaoke machine."

We look back and forth at each other like we don't have a choice as Dad finds the perfect spot to record.

Becca turns the karaoke off.

Emmanuel and I hold our guitars at the ready.

Oliver's fingers are poised over the keys.

Rocky clicks his drumsticks in a countdown, and the music begins. Ready or not, we shoot our first video, playing without the music backing us up. I just hope we sound good and don't kill the song. The music feels jerky, unnatural. Even Becca sounds like she ate a lemon before singing. There is no way we'll be accepted for the competition.

We hit the final note, and Rocky stops the cymbals with a hand grab. Silence reigns in the garage as Dad ends our recording session.

"You sound great. I think this will work."

"Can we see it first?" I set my guitar in its stand and go to Dad's side. We circle around, and he plays the recording back for us. He zoomed in on each of us when we played a feature part. We watch closely—everyone becomes their own critic.

"Look how I flinch on the bridge. I look like I stepped on Lego with my bare feet." I've actually done that before but have never seen what my face looks like.

The RUBBER BAND

"I almost skipped the second stanza. You can see the fear on my face." Emmanuel points to himself as the camera does a close-up.

"You look constipated!" Oliver grabs his stomach, giggling.

"Like you look or sound any better? I heard you fudge a few key notes." Emmanuel pokes Oliver in the ribs.

"Listen to the rasp in my voice. Now that's rock 'n' roll." Becca wastes no time elevating herself above the rest of us. Of course, she doesn't make any mistakes.

Rocky doesn't say a word.

"I'll submit the video to complete your application, and we'll be in business." Dad's voice sounds positive, but we aren't in the contest yet.

"Dad, are we going to keep practicing like we've been accepted?" Oliver makes a good point as we focus on Dad.

"Absolutely!" Dad doesn't hesitate to be positive. "I believe in you." Dad opens the door to leave but adds, "I believe in ALL of you."

Chapter Seventeen

Take-Over

Wednesday morning begins with our class taking a turn in a science hands-on assembly. Exhibits are set up throughout the multipurpose room for us to explore and play with. A giant glass ball in the center of the room has my attention. When you touch the ball, purple lightning bolts follow your fingers.

Searching the room for my friends, I notice Becca watching the giant bubble maker. If you stand still in the middle of the small round kiddie pool filled with bubble soap, the adult will carefully lift a Hula-Hoop from the pool, encasing you in a bubble. Oliver and Emmanuel join me.

"Do you think Becca will get in the pool?" Oliver whispers.

"No way. She's too much of a girly-girl to get messy," Emmanuel adds.

"I want to try being inside a giant bubble." The guys follow behind as I walk to the bubble pool.

We stand next to Becca. Four of my band members line up to watch the bubble rise and burst, sending slimy soap particles flying every direction. The upper grades and Rocky's class will take their turn at the assembly after we leave.

"Becca, are you going to try?" For some reason, I really want to see her encased in a bubble.

Becca turns her frowny face to me. "No way."

"What's the matter? Are you afraid the bubble splatter will get you all messy? A little too slimy for your brand-new

The RUBBER BAND

pedicure to take?" We snicker at Oliver's challenging words, except Becca. Her hands go to her hips, and her foot starts to tap.

"I'm not afraid. I have too much to do after school, and I can't get my clothes dirty."

"Yeah, you have to come hang out in a dirty, mice-infested, cob-webby garage with us for an hour!" Oliver's on a roll.

"Nope. I'm just here to watch." Becca steps back.

Her answer final, I get ready to step into the kiddie pool to take my turn at the bubble. I slip my shoes and socks off, hoping no one will breathe too deep lest they fall over from my odorous feet which I haven't cleaned in a few days.

"I DARE YOU!" Oliver bellows.

I can't believe my brother. He's asking for trouble.

"Move aside, Pinhead. It's my turn." Becca takes off her shoes and socks to reveal her pedicured toes all painted a bright orange polish with gold sparkles.

The adult running the bubbler helps Becca into the center like she is a breakable china doll. I don't see what the big deal is. It's only soap bubbles. Doesn't Becca ever take baths?

Slowly and carefully, an adult raises the Hula-Hoop until it creates a giant bubble tunnel surrounding Becca. A smirky grin crosses her face. We cheer for her success, but then she laughs. The air she breathes out makes the bubble wall pop, spritzing her and everyone close by with soapy goo.

Becca doesn't move.

Yep, she has bubble goo on her clothes, but her face wears a smile. She hops out and declares, "Your turn, Pinhead."

As the fragile bubble wall raises around me, I see the world from a new perspective. The inside of a soap bubble makes everything look rainbow wrinkled. Then in a split second, POP! The view returns to normal.

Needless to say, the experience is worth baring my stinky feet to the third grade.

"COOL!" Emmanuel and Oliver say together.

"Jinx! Poke! You owe me a Coke!" Oliver shoves his finger into Emmanuel's arm.

"Dude, really?" Emmanuel rubs the poke spot.

"Hey, have you guys tried the giant Plinko game?" Becca sits on a chair next to the pool, putting her socks and shoes back on.

"Not yet. But it looks like fun." I take a towel offered to me, sit on the floor, and dry the soap from between my toes, cleaning out the sock fuzzies stuck between them. Lifting my foot to my nose, I sniff. A strawberry scent wafts up my nose, and I sneeze.

"God bless you," Emmanuel said. "Plinko sounds like fun."

Becca follows us guys to the top of the Plinko board where we each take a turn. I drop my disc from the center, aiming for the one thousand-point mark in the bottom middle. We whoop and holler encouraging something lifeless to suddenly control its destiny, but it doesn't help. My disc drops into the zero points space.

"Nice try, Pinhead." Becca sets her disc free. Bouncing and bopping between the pegs, the disc lands dead center, one thousand points.

"Winner, winner, chicken dinner." Emmanuel waves his arms in the air.

Becca becomes our shadow at every science exhibit after that. We visit a magnet exhibit showing polar opposites and play with a giant fan and a floating beach ball. I lean over the fan, and my hair blows straight up. Soon everyone is doing the same thing. Becca's long dark hair flies up so high, she looks three feet taller.

The hour we have to explore goes by all too quickly. The entire class groans when Miss Crenshaw calls us to line up and return to the classroom.

The RUBBER BAND

I learned a lot of fun things about science. Science is full of observation and experimentation. One can say my putting a band together is much like a science experiment. I observed our newest band member today and came to a conclusion. Becca needs friends because she stuck to us like Velcro.

When Becca walks into a room, the entire place takes on a different feeling. The atmosphere changes from fun to all business. At our afternoon's practice, she proves it.

"I've put together CDs, memory sticks, and printed out the music for each of your parts." Becca hands us each a large yellowish envelope with our individual names in big black letters. "You'll find everything you need inside. My voice coach says the best thing we can do for our band is to work on our parts individually and then come together in a couple of days for a better sound."

Not one of us guys says a word.

A pain sharp as if I'd swallowed a handful of pushpins pricks my gut.

I thought I was the leader of the band.

"Wait a minute." I try to protest.

"Listen, Eddie." Becca hands me my envelope last. "I know what I'm doing here. I work with professionals all the time."

"What's that supposed to mean? We're just a kid band."

"True, but if we want to win, and trust me, we DO want to win, I have polled my resources and come up with a plan to put us in the front-running for first place. I can see the headline of the Sun Valley Times, 'Kid Band Takes Top Honors.'" Becca spreads her hands out like she can see the words on a giant movie theater marquee.

Things turn soft, and I feel like a tomato on a cutting board being sliced and diced until juice drips into a puddle. Heat floods my face as I press my hands against my sweaty cheeks.

"I am not a tomato!" The imaginary analogy in my mind gets the best of me and escapes in the volume of my voice.

The band's faces look like I caught them all at once in freeze tag. No one speaks. No one moves. I think I even scared the mouse to death, but I'd find out later he met his doom by eating poison disguised as Roquefort cheese.

Oliver and his quirky remark unfreeze the band.

"That's funny, 'cause your face looks as red as a tomato!"

"You don't get it!" My outside voice kicks in as I touch my cheeks to feel the heat. "This is my-My-MY! Band, BECCA! It's been MY idea since I sat in Principal Haymaker's office because YOU sent me there."

A couple weeks had passed since Bossy Becca tarnished my perfect-student record, without retaliation on my part. I'd pretty much stuffed my feelings inside, doing nothing. But this time she pushed the right button, setting off the ignition on my pent-up anger.

"I'm the one who saw the sign. I'm the one who asked Rocky to be our drummer and turn our just-fooling-around-with-music-in-the-garage into something special, and now YOU want to take over?"

Beads of sweat drip from my forehead onto the tip of my nose. I wipe the sweat on my sleeve and can feel the thirst for water rising in my throat.

No one says a word. I must have scared them. I scared myself.

Becca breaks the silence.

"What are you talking about? I never sent you to the principal's office. Miss Crenshaw did. She's the one to blame. NOT ME!"

The RUBBER BAND

Becca doesn't need to use the microphone to make her point.

Not one body part of the band members moves, except for their eyes darting back and forth between me and Becca.

"You played the drama queen and made a big deal out of a rubber band that Didn't. Even. Hit. Your. Face!" My voice is on the up escalator. "YOU got me into trouble for nothing."

"It wasn't nothing! You DID shoot the rubber band. You just have bad aim."

"Something I plan to get better at in the future."

Oliver snickers from behind his keyboard.

"This is my house, my garage, and MY BAND!"

With my face only inches away from the roaring dragon's breath, my heart pounds hard against my rib cage like it's Rocky kicking a beat on the bass drum. Why do I feel so strange and out of control? My mind clouds over, hiding any sunny ray of self-control. My fingers and toes tingle like they do when the blood circulation is cut off and slowly returns.

Before I can say anything angrier that makes no sense, Emmanuel does.

"Take a deep breath, Eddie. I think Becca's ideas are good, and we should take her advice. I for one don't want to get up in front of hundreds of strangers and be the joke of the contest."

My feet take me back a couple steps from Becca's face, but my heart holds its position. There's no way I'm going to let Bossy Becca take control. Who does she think she is anyway, throwing around her rich influence? Forgetting my conclusions about Becca from the science assembly, I refuse to back down, and I certainly don't want to be her friend.

"Eddie?" Rocky speaks from behind the drum set. "Our band doesn't belong to anyone. We're just a group of kids having fun. At least, we were."

Biting my lip, I know Rocky is right. I open my envelope and pull out the memory stick, fingering the label.

"Becca's put a lot of time into helping us out. She's part of the band 'that doesn't belong to anyone' too," Emmanuel adds his support.

Becca remains silent. For once.

"Emmanuel's right. If the professionals do it this way, we need to do it too. I don't want to get laughed off stage." Oliver has a point.

"Humiliation nation." Emmanuel drops his chin to his chest.

I stand in the middle of the garage. My gaze fixes on ants crawling randomly across the floor. I wish for the ants to assemble their army and haul me off to their anthill, pull me down the hole, and hide me from the world, at least from the people in the garage. No one likes to be embarrassed. No matter if I am an angry chopped tomato in a salad of cloudy-brain emotions, the band has a point.

"Okaaaay," I mumble. Heaving a deep, long sigh, I concede to Bossy Becca. "How do we do this?"

A smile as big as the Grand Canyon crosses Becca's face.

"The band is going to take a few days off. Practice your individual parts over the weekend, and when we meet on Monday afternoon, I promise there will be a huge difference in how we sound. When it's our turn to play on that stage in two weeks, we'll be nothing short of amazing!"

Two weeks.

That's all the time we have to perfect one song. My panic button goes off, and I excuse myself, running to the bathroom—not to throw-up, I really had to pee. I return with a bottle of water for everyone. Two bottles for me since the desert in the back of my mouth is begging for a flash flood.

The RUBBER BAND

　　While I was gone, Becca's plan grew bigger. She's arranged with her voice music coach for us to have individual lessons. The guys agree. My opinion doesn't feel like it matters anymore, so I pick up my guitar and wait for Becca to push play on the karaoke machine.

　　We play through the song three times before Albert comes to pick up Becca. To me, we don't need individual work. I think we're coming together just fine. Becca lives up to her nickname when she takes charge, and I truly am a pinhead to let her. For now and forever, I'll hear about this until I die. If it were possible, I'd time travel back to the classroom, to the moment before I shot the rubber band and ignore Becca instead.

CHAPTER EIGHTEEN

My Turn

Friday morning, my stomach wakes me up early. I think I'm going to hurl or maybe I'm just overly hungry. Today is my turn to have a private lesson with the music coach. I didn't sleep much. Last night, I woke up four times to go to the bathroom and get a drink of water. All this water drinking and then thinking about how Becca took over the band making us take private lessons kept me awake.

I pour a bowl of my favorite sugar cereal, grab a cup for orange juice, and suck everything down in less than five minutes like I haven't eaten in months. Whenever I eat like this, Mom says I'm growing. Today must be a growing day. I'm still hungry, so I pour another bowl of cereal, emptying the box.

As lead guitarist for the band, I waste no time listening to my part, over and over and over until I can whistle it in my sleep. Maybe that's the reason for no sleep?

Isn't the guitar player usually the head of the band?

Research had probably been done on the subject, so I decide to look up rock 'n' roll band leaders on the internet when I get home from school. Friday means no homework, and I have an hour until the music coach shows up. I'll do the research then.

In class, working on my math page, the music won't stop playing in my head. I can't think through its noise. The problems blur, so I lean closer to them and squint. It isn't my

The RUBBER BAND

best work, but for now, the only work I really want to do is on the band.

"Eddie?" Miss Crenshaw calls my name. "Are you feeling okay?"

Apparently, I look sick or something with my head leaning down on my desk.

I straighten up and answer, "I'm fine." But, a few minutes later, I am off to the restroom. Maybe I'm catching something? My stomach reminds me of how I woke up, and I almost lose my breakfast leaning over the toilet.

Not a good way to start a weekend.

At recess time, I don't feel up to playing dynamite ball. As much as the guys beg, after drinking my juice box and eating a couple of cookies, I sprawl on my back on the picnic table bench, close my eyes, and absorb the sun's heat. From there, I can hear the girls playing tag run past screaming, the banging of the basketball on the court, and the whooshing of the tree branches in the wind.

"If you stay there long enough, one of the birds is going to drop a load on you." Rocky plops on the only part of the bench my body doesn't occupy. "What's with you, Eddie?"

Sitting up put me in a better place to answer, but I don't say a word.

"First, you go all control-freaky at the band, and now, you don't want to play ball like you always do. Are you changing your mind about the contest? Are you backing out? After all the trouble you went through to get us weirdos together, have you lost it?"

Is this coming from Rocky?

Again, I don't know what to say. Words jumble in my brain but won't make a complete sentence.

"Your dad bought me a drum set, so I could play in the band. I can't let him down."

True, Dad and Mom had been behind this idea since I shared it with them. I don't want to let them down either. I'm just not feeling so good at the moment, but before I can finally get words out of my mouth to explain, Rocky leaves. He puts his earbuds in and walks the school perimeter once more like he doesn't have any friends to hang out with.

I know differently.

After recess comes spelling. I love spelling. Usually I get one hundred percent correct on the twenty-five words each week. After the test, Miss Crenshaw writes next week's words on the board, and we copy them into our homework journals to study.

I'm ready with my journal open and a sharpened pencil poised in my hand, but I can't get my brain to focus. When Miss Crenshaw turns to face us, revealing next week's words, I can't read one of them. They fuzz together like a blurry smudge. I have to squint my eyes like Dad does when he forgets to wear his reading glasses. Squinting doesn't help. Maybe I need glasses?

I raise my hand. Miss Crenshaw comes to my side.

"May I get closer to the board?"

This is totally out of character for me, so when I sit crisscross applesauce on the floor closer to the board with my journal and pencil, I get some weird looks and hear the questioning whispers of the other kids.

As we are dismissed for lunch, Miss Crenshaw asks me to chat with her. My fuzzy brain plunges deep into its grey matter trying to retrieve from my memory banks what I could have done wrong.

"Eddie, I'm sending this note home to your parents. It's important they read it as soon as possible. Don't leave it in your folder or backpack, okay?"

I take the envelope, staring at the floor.

"Please don't worry, you're not in trouble."

The RUBBER BAND

Well, there's a relief.

"Just make sure they get it tonight, okay?"

"Okay, Miss Crenshaw. Can I go to lunch now? I'm starving."

"Of course, but I'll know if you forgot about the note if your parents don't call me."

My curiosity wants to sneak the envelope out to lunch with me and secretly open it, but I can feel Miss Crenshaw's eyes watching. I tuck the note in my backpack's side pocket, grab my lunch box, and join the guys at our usual, bird-poop-covered table.

Peanut butter and grape jelly has never tasted so good. But as I dive into my lunch like a stray dog on a steak, I notice Rocky sitting at his old spot, far away from us. Emmanuel and Oliver aren't saying anything, so I just keep devouring my lunch, sucking the apple juice box until it implodes. I put the box up for the three-point shot into the blurry trash can and don't see if I've made the shot or not.

When yard duty excuses us, a member of the environmental club walks by, picks up the empty juice box, and without hesitation, calls me an earth-killer. The guys leave me sitting alone munching the last of my orange slices. They blur off into the distance to the basketball court, and I fight the feeling to lay down on the bench again. Instead, I go to the water fountain, take a long drink, and make my way to the library. I can do my research now instead of waiting until I get home.

Typing "famous band leads that play guitar" I hope to stop my nagging thoughts about Becca's takeover. An article of the ten top guitar leads pops up, and along with it, a list of lead singers from bands I've never heard of, but I bet my parents have. One guitarist for the Beatles, John Lennon, wore round lens glasses and a headband around his shaggy, shoulder-length hair. As much as I want to be the leader, I refuse to wear headbands like a girl.

Next, I peruse the list of lead singers, which is equally as long. Both lists describe the great lyrics and music the singers have written. As I read further, I find the reason many of the great bands break up is because one or more of the members want to go solo, on their own.

Should I fight Bossy Becca for control of the band or give in to her ideas for improvement?

Will my fighting to be the leader cause my band to break up before playing our first gig?

Am I the ONE?

I'm feeling like the kid who put his finger through the perfectly smooth frosted wedding cake, ruining it before the photos are taken just because he wants a taste.

The facts are clear.

Who's in charge doesn't matter as long as the band makes music.

Rocky's words plug my disconnected brain back into its socket.

I'll apologize to the band at our practice on Monday. But for today, I'll just smile my way through my private lesson to appease Becca's need to control everything and hope for the best.

As we arrive home, Dad waits at the front door, waving a white piece of paper like a flag in the wind.

"Great news!" Dad looks like a kid on Christmas morning, waiting to open presents. "I got the official email notice this morning and almost ran to school to tell everyone. The band is in the contest!"

The Rubber Band

I drop my backpack. "No way! No way! No way!" I jump up and down and spin around while jumping, I look like a pogo stick.

"We're in?" Oliver squawks.

"That's what it says." Dad waves the paper again, and we take turns reading it.

"We've got to tell the others."

Telling the others one by one using Face2Face, I am excited and enthused like I was when we first started this project. Everyone reacts differently. Emmanuel falls to the floor like he's dead. Rocky smiles and pumps his fist up and down. Becca is working with her tutor, so Albert says he'll let her know once she finishes. I bet she celebrates in a crazy way too.

Now it's time to get serious.

Oliver disappears to our room as I wait in the garage, my guitar in hand, staring at the sheet music in front of me. The notes look like the spelling words, fuzzing together like watercolors on a canvas.

"Eddie." The sound of Mom's voice brings my attention to the open door. A tall, scrawny man with a long, grey, braided ponytail follows behind her. "This is Mr. Zee. He's here to give you your lesson."

I can tell from the tone of Mom's voice she doesn't want to leave me alone with someone who looks like they stepped off the happy bus from the 60s. I secretly wonder why he is called by the last letter of the alphabet.

Mr. Zee holds his hand out and grips mine like a vice from Dad's toolbox.

"Nice to meet you, Eddie. Congratulations on getting your band into the contest."

I wish it was MY band. I'll deal with that feeling later.

"You must know by now the guitarist plays a very important part in the band. He's the leader, and the energy level of every band is set by a great leader."

How does this guy know what I've been thinking?

"So, let's get started and see what you've got."

Standing in front of the music, I struggle through the first few bars, squinting. I stop and jerk at every bar because I have to keep looking back and forth from the music to where my jumbled fingers are placed on the guitar. The sound I emit is like I've never touched a guitar in my life—a baby plunking on the keys of a piano just to make noise. When I finally finish, heat rises in my cheeks, sweat beads on my forehead, and my heart feels like it hits the cement floor. Though I still wonder about his name, I can't face Mr. Zee.

"Eddie. It's never easy to play for a stranger. I know you've practiced, and I know you're better than what I just heard."

Mr. Zee stands so close to me, when I look up to his face, I see his sparkly blue eyes behind the John Lennon glasses. At least, he's not blurry.

"I notice you are squinting a lot. Do you wear glasses?" He peers at me over the rims of his rounded frames.

"No." His question reminds me of the note Miss Crenshaw sent home.

OOPS!

The note is still in the side pocket of my backpack. I'll give it to Mom first thing after I finish my private music lesson.

The RUBBER BAND

"Hm." Mr. Zee holds his chin in a thoughtful pose. "Let's try playing with headphones. You listen and play along, and I'll hear just you."

Playing through goes easier not having to read blurry music. When I finish, Mr. Zee's grin wrinkles his half-shaved face like a porcupine smile.

"Wonderful! I knew you could do it!"

There is no heat in my cheeks or sweat on my brow this time when my eyes meet his. If this is what confidence feels like, I crave more.

"You don't need the sheet music. You can play by heart."

"With my heart?"

"Yes, with your heart. Put your heart and soul into it."

"I don't understand, Mr. Zee?"

"Oh, I think you do. Let me show you."

Mr. Zee takes my guitar and turns on the karaoke machine. As the music plays, he closes his eyes, strums through the beginning, and then runs around the garage in unison with the beat while tied to a cord and amplifier. I think he's going to tangle and fall face-first onto the cement, but somehow, he moves with grace, gliding across the floor. I can't tell where the guitar stops and his body begins. When the final note sounds, he drops to his knees, holding the guitar by the neck while pointing his finger to the sky.

So, that's what it means to put your heart and soul into something. Haven't I been dreaming of that style all along? I guess I've been holding back.

"So, what do you think, Eddie?"

"I'll show you what I think." Taking my guitar back, I play "Born to be Wild" like I'd been born a rock star. The audience is roaring their approval. Girls in the front row scream my name. Flowers and other things are tossed onto stage. Security guards push back the people reaching so close they'd get my sweat dripped on them or be hit by spit catapulted from my carefree singing, all while I dance about the stage, giving the show they love.

"WOW! Eddie! That's it! You've got it! Whatever was going through your head, keep it going. That's what heart and soul is all about—being free and letting the music take you to places you can only dream of."

If I could see my face in a mirror, I'm sure my face won't fit because a giant smile stretches my face muscles to what feels like a mile beyond the mirror's frame.

"We'll need to get you a wireless, so you have more freedom. I can arrange to have one for your next group practice."

I play through two more times, adding more heart and soul, until my hour is up, and Oliver comes to take his turn with Mr. Zee. I'm having fun and don't want to stop. I wish I can take Oliver's lesson time. I'm also dying to ask my instructor a question that has nothing to do with music.

"Um, Mr. Zee." My voice lacks the confidence of my guitar playing. "Is Zee short for something, or is your real name Mr. Zee?"

Finally. Relief from my annoying curiosity.

Mr. Zee's porcupine smile comes back.

"I got the nickname Zee back when I was your age. It's short for Zekowski. To this day, that's what I'm remembered for."

I guess nicknames make a lasting impression, only I don't want to be remembered as "pinhead" for the rest of my life.

CHAPTER NINETEEN

TAKE DOWN

Turns out I didn't have to worry too much about Miss Crenshaw's note being a bad thing. She is concerned I might need glasses since I couldn't see the spelling words on the board. It suggested my parents make an eye exam appointment as soon as possible. She is such a thoughtful teacher. I wish she could be my teacher every year.

Since Dad is a doctor, he didn't waste time calling his friend who specializes in kids with seeing problems. I have an appointment with him after school today. Dad says I'll get eye drops to make my pupils big for the eye doctor to see the blood vessels in back of my eye. I wonder if he can see my brain cells too.

I worry all weekend about getting glasses. I'm already teased for being smart and having a pointy-shaped head. Wearing glasses will give kids more to pick on me, making life worse. If I have to get glasses, maybe I can choose some cool frames like John Lennon wore, and one day when I am a famous rock 'n' roll star, my cool shades will be iconic.

Gulping down almost a gallon of grape juice with my usual sugar cereal breakfast. I think about our band practice today and my plan to apologize and set things right. I also wonder how the rest of everyone else's private lessons have gone, hoping Becca's take-over had been a good thing after all.

The RUBBER BAND

The smile from my unforgettable lesson on Friday is still on my face when I float through the door of the third-grade classroom. I doubt I had frowned all weekend. Happy people often talk about being on cloud nine. I'm not sure what that means. But since breakfast, I did feel like I was walking in the clouds.

Becca is first to finish her math and get to games. I haven't even finished the first problem when Oliver sits down to be her partner.

Why is my brain taking hours to do the problems that usually take me minutes to finish?

I press so hard my pencil's lead breaks. Getting a new pencil out, I glance up to find most of the class has finished and are playing math games. I'll be stuck with a partner who doesn't know their math facts if I don't hurry up and finish, but I can't figure out the problems. I've done double-digit addition many times and know how to carry numbers, but at the moment, the numbers feel like they weigh a thousand pounds, and there is no way I can carry them correctly.

I close my eyes trying to find an answer in the dark recess of my brain. It doesn't help and only makes me tired. Maybe if I just I lay my head down on my desk ...

Voices ask mumbled questions, poking, prodding, lifted to a bed and covered in warmth, straps pull tight, bumpy rolling ride, red flashing lights, sirens roaring, the smell of a freshly opened Band-Aid box, moving quickly, a strange voice, "You're going to be all right, kid." Every bodily sense is at work begging for attention. It must be another crazy dream.

Beep.
Beep.
Beep.

Opening my eyes, I'm no longer at my desk worrying about math problems. Instead, I'm lying on my back, staring at a ceiling tiled in squares that look like someone poked random holes into them with a pencil. The bed has bars like a jungle gym, and tubes are coming from my arms. My eyes follow the tubes to a pole holding bags filled with clear liquid, slowly dripping. Lights blink on machines next to the bed. One beeps continuously.

Where am I? Is this just my crazy dream getting crazier?

I want to pinch myself like they say to do to figure out if you are dreaming or not, but when I try, tape and tubes stop me. A curtain attached to the ceiling by hooks on a metal runner, ripples back and forth. I can see people with white running shoes walking on the other side.

Beep.
Beep.
Beep.

The machine continues to make a constant annoying sound.

The curtain is pulled back by a woman wearing purple scrubs decorated with cartoon dogs as doctors. She comes to the bedside and pushes a button on the machine, silencing its cries.

"Welcome back, Mr. Taylor." The woman examines the other machines.

"You're not Miss Crenshaw."

"Of course not, sweetheart, I'm Norie, your nurse."

The RUBBER BAND

I look this Norie nurse-person over and figure I'm still dreaming.

"I'm here to take your vitals, and then I'll let your parents know you're awake." She pushes a button, and the head of the bed raises up. I sit forward, and she tucks a pillow behind my back.

"Where am I?" I manage to ask before Norie runs a thermometer over my forehead.

Norie puts something around my arm, fastening it with Velcro. The band tightens and squeezes so hard as it hums, I think my hand is going to fall off.

"Normal temp, that's good, and this is Memorial Hospital children's ward." The thermometer beeps, and she pulls it out, smiling. "Normal. That's good."

The wrap around my arm deflates just in time before my head explodes.

"Blood pressure is excellent. Let's see if we can get your blood sugar to do the same." Norie pushes another button at the head of the bed. "The button I pushed will let the doctor know you're ready to be seen."

Hospital, doctor, nurse, I'm not in third grade anymore.

What happened? Why am I here? My stomach tightens up. Tears fill my eyes, and, before I can stop them, they spill down my cheeks non-stop like Niagara Falls.

A hand pulls the curtain back, and Mom rushes to my side. Despite all the medical wires and tubes connected to me, she scoops me in her arms and squeezes me tight. No words are spoken. I cry until the falls dry up. Mom doesn't mind all the nose goobers dripping on her flower-print blouse, and I don't mind hers dripping on whatever it is I am wearing tied up at the back of my neck.

When I finally let go of Mom, I see Dad sitting at the bottom of the bed, holding his chin in one hand.

"Hey there, son."

I think I smile at Dad's words, but millions of questions swirl in my mind that need answers. My stomach is still tight—fear instead of food, filling its empty space. I grab Mom again and hug her, longing for security, something familiar, to keep me steady.

Dad stands as a man in a long white coat shakes his hand. I relax my grip on Mom but keep holding her hand.

"Edison, it's great to see you awake. I'm Dr. Klekman, and I'm in charge of getting you back on your feet, ready to face life in new ways, once you're healthy again."

Dr. Klekman held his hand out to me, but I just squeeze Mom's hand harder.

"Sorry, I know it's hard to shake a doctor's cold hand when yours is connected to all the machines. We have a lot to talk about and teach you while the medicine gets you better. I'll be checking in with you several times every day. We'll be best friends before you leave."

Best friends?

The band!

Do they know where I am?

Do they know what is happening?

"I think you need some time with your parents. I'll return later." Dr. Klekman leaves me staring at Dad while I squeeze Mom's hand tighter.

"I'm sorry, son. As a doctor, I should've seen this coming." Dad's usually steady voice trembles.

"What's going on, Daddy?" My own voice quavers.

A tear drips from Dad's eye. This must be serious. Am I dying?

"Eddie, you have diabetes." Dad wipes his tear with a handkerchief.

"I'm going to DIE?" I squeeze Mom's hand so tight her fingers might fall off.

The RUBBER BAND

He did say DIE, didn't he? I don't want to die, at least not before my tenth birthday!

Dad sits on the end of the bed once more.

"You're not going to die. Diabetes is a manageable disease. It's going to take some adjustments and changes, some you probably won't like, but we will be there to help with everything."

I don't hear him say much after the word disease.

On the wall ahead of me is a round, analog clock. I can hear it ticking but can't see the hands or the numbers. Not being able to see the clock reminds me of the spelling words I couldn't see, and the math problems on the paper I couldn't figure out.

"I fell asleep on my math problems." It's the first thing I can remember.

"Yes, you did." Mom pulls me closer.

"I couldn't finish my morning wake-up work, and everyone was playing math games. I'm usually done before Becca, but then." I stop talking because I realize I don't know the details of how I ended up here.

"Miss Crenshaw says you can take your time on any work you miss." Dad fills me in on what's going on. "She just wants you to get better, as I'm sure your classmates do too."

Nurse Norie comes back announcing she has to test my blood sugar, so Mom gets up to stand by Dad. I have no idea what Nurse Norie means until she takes my left pointer finger, cleans it with a rubbing alcohol pad, lets it dry, squeezes the end of my finger until it turns bright red then …

"OWWWW!"

The needle poke brings tears to my eyes as Nurse Norie puts a drop, OF MY BLOOD, on a strip poking out of a thing that looks like an MP3 player.

"I'm sorry, Eddie. But you'll have to get used to this routine. It's how we determine the amount of insulin to give you by the number that comes on the screen." She shows me the MP3 player thing, and sure enough, the small screen blinked 595.

"Is that good?"

"Much better than when you arrived. The first time we tested your blood, the number was too high to register on the meter. Your blood sugar is still pretty high and has to get much lower. The lower the number goes, the sooner you'll be going home." She presses a few buttons on one of the machines connected to me.

Thoughts of all the video games I've played come to mind, and I can't help but wonder why a lower number is better.

"Hopefully, tomorrow you'll be learning more about diabetes and how to manage it, but until then, we need to get your blood sugar number down to at least one hundred. That will take some time."

I can't see what time it is on the wall clock, but my tummy growling makes everyone giggle.

"I'd say someone's hungry?" Nurse Norie checks one of the bags hanging on the pole next to the bed. "Can it possibly be you?"

I nod yes.

"I'll bring your dinner in a few minutes. Monday's menu is usually roast beef, mashed potatoes and gravy with a side of green beans, and sugar free Jell-O for dessert. How does that sound?"

I don't care what's for dinner. I'm so hungry I'd eat my shoes if I were wearing them. What am I wearing anyway?

"I'm really thirsty. Can I have a drink of water?"

"Sure, sweetie. This pitcher of water is for you and you alone. I need to keep track of how much you drink." She pours water into a cup that matches the mustard yellow colored pitcher. "Here you go."

The RUBBER BAND

I guzzle without stopping, take a breath, and say, "I need to pee."

At that moment, I feel something attached to a private place. Nurse Norie glances at Dad and Mom.

"That's something I need to keep track of too. You won't be able to get out of bed because of the monitors, so you have a catheter. It's a tube that allows you to go pee, right where you are, whenever you feel the need. For now, we'll leave and give you some privacy."

Nurse Norie takes Mom and Dad out of the room leaving me to think about the process. She's right. I don't have much of a choice since I can't get out of bed. Good thing I have to go really bad, because if I had to think about going, no matter if my bladder exploded, I probably wouldn't go.

A few minutes later Mom and Dad return, arm in arm. Nurse Norie sets my plastic covered dinner on a tray table that slides across the bed. She picks up a bag hanging from the bar on the side of the bed, and after studying it for a second, hangs the bag back, makes notes, then washes her hands. She pulls the plastic off my dinner. I know Mom is glad Nurse Norie washed her hands before opening everything up to show me what I am being served.

"Eddie." I eyeball the food on the tray table in front of me while Mom talks. "I'll be staying the night with you, but I need to go home and bring some things back. Is there anything you might like to have from home to make you more comfortable?" Mom smiles and tussles my hair.

The only thing I really want from home is my guitar, but I won't be able to play it in a hospital, tied to all the machines, and peeing in a bag.

Is this DIE-abetes thing going to stop me from playing guitar?

With no idea what is going to happen next, I fear the worst.

I can't possibly go through with the talent contest having gotten this DIE-abetes thing. I'll have to drop out of the band. No time to get a replacement lead guitarist.

My dream has been taken down and will have to die, like in DIE-abetes.

Despite the sick feeling this thought gives me, I can't deny my hunger. I stab the roast beef with the plastic fork and take a bite.

CHAPTER TWENTY

LIVE OR DIE-ABETES

I've always heard a rumor they feed you gelatin in the hospital, and now I know the rumor to be a truth. The fact is, however, the gelatin is the most flavorful part of the meal. The green beans come in second with the gravy in dead last. Apparently, the cook doesn't know what salt or seasoning is.

Mom returns bringing my favorite blanket, pillow, and some comic books. A folded bed is wheeled in for her to sleep on. I have no idea what time it is since I still can't read the clock on the wall, but it must be late because I can see the city lights glowing through the window in the dark night.

We watch cartoons until I get sleepy. Mom pushes the control button, and the head of my bed lays down. I'm not sure how I'll be able to sleep, attached to everything, but Mom tucks me in and sits next to me. She leaves the TV on, and we watch late into the evening until my eyelids feel like sandy weights are pulling them shut.

I wake to a silent room in the darkness of the night. Moonlight shines on Mom curled up, sleeping a few feet away from me. The privacy curtain between my bed and the door ripples, and a different nurse comes to my side, pulls my hand from under the covers, and then …

"OWW!" I squawk, tears fill my eyes.

She'd jabbed my finger and now squeezes it until blood drops onto the test strip. "You better get used to this, kid."

Get used to it? What does that mean?

The RUBBER BAND

This nurse says nothing else to me. I figure it's because the hospital needs to be quiet, like a library, especially at night when everyone is sleeping. That same nurse wakes me up a gazillion times to poke my finger and squeeze out my blood. I lose count of how often she makes me bleed. I think she's really a vampire dressed as a nurse. IF I wake up ALIVE in the morning, I'll have to tell the truth about her to Dr. Klekman, unless he's a vampire too!

To my relief, my eyes open to morning sunshine. I must not have been sucked dry of blood because I'm not dead. However, I'm still attached to all the machines. What happened yesterday wasn't a dream after all. The smell of eggs and bacon somewhere makes my tummy grumble, and I hope the breakfast tray will be sitting in front of me soon.

"Your mom is getting coffee and her own breakfast." Nurse Norie brings scrambled eggs, bacon, toast, milk, and a bowl of oatmeal.

"Before you eat anything, you must first test your blood sugar. I'll do it for you until you feel up to trying yourself." She gets my finger ready. "I hear you're a guitar player. Tell me what you play."

"I play lead in my," remembering the apology I have yet to give, I rephrase my sentence. "I play lead guitar in OUR garage band."

Nurse Norie is sneaky. While I tell her about our band, she pokes my finger, and I don't squawk or feel a thing. Thank goodness the vampire's shift was over.

"Your number has improved. You're in the low 300s."

Once again, I think the higher the number, the bigger win.

"I don't understand the number thing." I stuff a strange looking piece of bacon in my mouth.

"The lower your blood sugar numbers are, the healthier you'll feel. It's not like getting high score in a video game.

But you'll learn more about diabetes management before you leave the hospital, and then you'll be learning and adjusting for the rest of your life, or until there's a cure."

I would love a cure right now, but right this minute, I'm hungry, and my eggs are really dry and tasteless.

"Do you think I can get some ketchup for my eggs?"

"I can check the kitchenette, but we'll have to count the carbs as ketchup has sugar. You'll be learning more about food when the nutritionist visits. Unfortunately, hospital food is pretty bland. They purposely keep the stuff out that gives food flavor to make sure patients are filled with nutrients that won't harm or hinder their way back to good health."

Nurse Norie sees me make a funny face as I bite into the bacon. In my opinion, the cook must have mistaken leather for the meat because it's like chewing on my summer sandal.

When Mom returns, she tells me Dad will come by later. He'll be at the hospital visiting his patients or doing what he calls "his rounds."

After I finish breakfast, Nurse Norie puts a video on about die-abetes. The video talks about how to manage die-abetes daily by using the glucose monitor. That's the thing I gave blood to, all night. The video shows various ways of treating die-abetes, but all of them involve bleeding and needles, electronic devices, and tubes connected to my body.

Turning off the TV, Nurse Norie brings me an orange, a needle, and a bottle of liquid.

"Before you can leave the hospital, you must show us you can do the minimum required to treat your diabetes. You'll have to use the glucometer and give yourself a shot."

She takes the bottle, and with the plunger on the needle, pulls out to the number twenty. She pushes the air from the needle into the bottle. I watch as the bubbles rise to the top.

The RUBBER BAND

"It's a vacuum void, so you must fill the bottle with the same amount of air as the amount of medicine you need to take out."

This sounds like science class to me.

She draws out the liquid to the number twenty again.

"Make sure there are no bubbles in the needle." She flicks the needle, and little bubbles float to the top, then she presses the plunger until the last air bubble escapes the needle.

Nurse Norie takes the orange in her hands. "It's best to practice with saline and fruit." Without hesitation, she plunges the needle into the peel and pushes the plunger down. The poor orange didn't see it coming.

"Now, it's your turn." Nurse Norie offers me the orange.

My stomach twists up. Ever since I can remember, I've hated needles. Most of the time you get a shot poked into you so abruptly, it scares you, and then there is the pain and reaction to the vaccine like fevers and sore muscles. I'm starting to feel sorry for the orange.

Following Nurse Norie's example, I fill the needle. But, as I hold the orange and picture it being my own skin, my hand trembles. Niagara Falls returns to my cheeks. The orange drops from my hand and rolls across the floor.

"You're going to be okay, Eddie." Mom comes to my side and holds me in her arms, ignoring the tubes, letting me get snot all over her shirt again.

"Yes, Eddie, things will get better, just take your time. I'll be back later this afternoon to see how you're doing. In the meantime, when you feel up to it, practice."

Her kind voice assures me she doesn't like this anymore than I do. She definitely isn't a vampire making me bleed every hour.

Miss Crenshaw comes in to visit me while I'm eating lunch and watching a not-so-clear cartoon channel. She brings a giant homemade card the entire class made and signed. Some of the students drew pictures beside their names. In the bottom corner is a picture drawn by Oliver and Emmanuel of the band. In big letters I can read without being blurry, they had written "Roadkill" by the drummer and "Becca the Boss" over the stick figure holding what looks like a microphone.

For the first time since I came to the hospital, I laugh.

"I'm glad you're smiling." Mom comes to my side to peek at the card. "Thank you for bringing this, Miss Crenshaw."

"The entire class is so worried, I told them I'd take my lunch break to come and see you and then bring them back a report on how you're doing. The giant card was Becca's idea."

I search the card for Becca's name and find it under a drawing of a flower resembling a snapdragon. Her drawing reminds me of flowers at Grandma's house. We used to pull the snapdragons off the stem and squish the petals together, popping it open to look like a roaring mouth. How appropriate that "dragon-breath" Becca drew a snapdragon, and I dreamed she was a dragon.

"I'll let them all know you're getting better. Please don't worry about catching up on the work you miss. There's no doubt in my mind you'll be just fine, academically and physically. Just get well soon." Miss Crenshaw pats my hand and leaves as I try to read every word of the giant card.

When I finish, Mom pins the card to a half corkboard, half whiteboard under the round thing on the wall that is looking more like a clock, but I still can't read the time.

As promised, Nurse Norie returns early in the afternoon offering me a stuffed brown teddy bear dressed in a T-shirt and overalls.

The RUBBER BAND

"His name is Grin N. Bearit, but you can name him anything you want. He's a gift from the local diabetes association. They give every child this bear to help them cope with diabetes." She lifts his pant legs to reveal a red patch on one leg and a green one on the other. "He also has patches on his arms, bum, and belly, all places where he can inject his insulin. But best of all, he is wearing an insulin pump which you'll be wearing before you leave."

I examine him thoroughly. I want to see every inch of this die-abetic teddy bear.

"What's this for?" I point out a bracelet on one of his furry wrists.

"It's his medical bracelet that identifies him as a diabetic in case of emergencies. You'll get one too before you're sent home."

I'll definitely think of a better name for the bear.

"Have you been practicing on the orange? We teach you how to use needles as a backup in case the pump malfunctions."

"Nope." The orange sits next to a needle and bottle on the little dresser stand by my bed. So far, I'm not as good at this die-abetes thing like I am at schoolwork. If I don't get over my fear of needles, I'll have to live in the hospital forever.

"That's okay." She doesn't sound disappointed. "There's a lot to learn about diabetes. New technology is always changing its management, so you'll be learning for the rest of your life or until there's a cure. I bet you feel like this is too much information all at once."

She got that one right. My mind is getting clearer, but there is too much information to think straight.

"I'll show you how once more, in case you forgot." Nurse Norie is really sweet, but the poor orange takes five shots from her before she gives me a turn. "You're a smart young man. Before you know, it'll become routine. You'll manage like it's your second skin." She sets up the glucose monitor. "I'd like to set a goal of getting you to test your own blood sugar by tomorrow. Then we can get on to better things when I introduce you to the insulin pump."

"You're getting an insulin pump? Way to go, Eddie!" Dad strolls in with a get-well balloon and a wrapped box that rattles when he moves it. "That's fantastic. It's the best in technology to treat diabetes. You look much better than when I saw you last." He sets the box on my lap and tussles my hair. "How do you feel?"

Whenever an adult asks a kid that question, we all have the standard answer, "Fine."

"I think he's overwhelmed, but his blood sugar is coming down nicely and should be within normal range by tomorrow morning." Nurse Norie has a much better answer than I do.

I shake the box. It's definitely the Lego building set I wanted for Christmas. I tear the box open, without thinking to ask permission first.

"I know you've wanted this set for a long time. I thought it would give you motivation to do what needs to be done to get discharged and home where we'll build it together." Dad's right. I want nothing more than to get out of the hospital but just can't leave until I pass a few tests harder than the ones at school.

"I've got a few more patients to see, but when I finish, I'm going to spend the night with you, so Mom can go home and get some rest. It's not easy sleeping on a hospital cot."

"My back can use a rub," Mom says, embracing Dad and smacking him with a long kiss right on the lips!

"EWWW!" Some things never change.

The RUBBER BAND

Dad is going to take Mom out to dinner and then home, leaving me, the bear that has no name, and the orange, watching the cartoon channel again. I'm staring at vintage cartoon hour, and I'm bored with the unfamiliar. I spy the orange and the needle. It feels like they are begging me to practice with them, so I turn off the TV and give them my full attention.

Drawing up the saline is the easy part. If only I can jab the needle into the orange like Nurse Norie does. I raise the syringe and poise it above the unsuspecting fruit. My heart races. I feel like the Cowardly Lion in The Wizard of Oz, searching for courage. He found courage somehow. Thoughts of sleeping in my own bed, going back to school, and practicing with the band, run through my mind. If I get the basics down, I'll be putting my Lego blocks together at home real soon. I close my eyes, wishing I were home right now.

"Hey, Eddie. What are you doing?" Emmanuel's voice is the sweetest sound I've heard all day.

Forgetting the about-to-be-skewered orange, I nearly jump out of bed to hug my friend, except that would be ugly, not to mention it would make a wet, smelly mess if the bag-thing came undone.

Emmanuel, Oliver, and Becca stand at the end of my bed. Rocky leans, arms folded, one foot pressing against the clock and corkboard wall. He reminds me of an iconic picture I'd seen from the fifties of James Dean.

"It's awesome to see you guys." I can feel my face-hurting smile.

"You look like a science experiment." Oliver points to my IV pole and all the tubes attached to me.

"Thanks for the card. Miss Crenshaw told me it was your idea, Becca."

Becca's quietness reminds me of the apology I had yet to give.

"I wanted to tell you guys something on Monday at practice, but this die-abetes thing stopped me."

"Are you contagious?" Oliver fingers the IV pole, quizzically.

All three of them take a step back from the bed. Rocky just shakes his head.

"Do you think they would let you in here if I was?"

The three of them come back to the bedside.

"What did you want to tell us?" Emmanuel studies the blinking machines monitoring my every bodily function.

"I wanted to say I'm sorry."

Rocky moves off the wall and closer to me.

"I've been very selfish."

The only sound is the muffled voices from the nurse's station.

"The last time we played together, I made the contest all about me. It's not about me but a team effort. Each of us brings our own talent that on our own won't matter a whole lot. But now …" I don't know how to tell them I am leaving the band.

"Yeah, we knew you weren't happy." Emmanuel's words rescue me for the moment. "But what good is it to get mad at you? We all have the same dream of winning the contest. You just never thought we did. It's going to be so cool to play in front of a huge audience and let the whole world know who we are!"

"He's right. It's our dream too," Oliver adds.

I roll the orange around in my hand, heave a sigh, and fight back tears.

"The dream is over. I've ruined it by getting sick. I won't be able to play guitar with all the holes in my fingers from testing my blood sugar. Worse yet, I could get too much insulin and pass out while playing on stage. I'm sorry guys. I can't do it. I'm out."

Four voices all at once break into a negative chorus of a tune I've never heard before. It sounds like, "What? Don't, never, wait, how can you?" all garbled together.

Rocky whistles. I'm sure the nurses don't appreciate it, but everyone stops talking. "Eddie, you can't let this diabetes thing stop you. It may be the worst thing that has ever happened to you, but I think you can still live with it." Rocky pulls the chair close to the bed and sits. His piercing eyes stare me down. His voice grows quiet, like we are the only two in the room.

"The only way to survive the bad notes life sings to you is to keep playing until the music is in tune again."

Wow! Did that come from Rocky, the kid I used to avoid? What he said makes sense in a wise, old man kind of way. Everyone stares at me waiting for my response. I have a big choice to make.

"Speaking of letting the whole world know who we are." Becca's hands are on her hips like she has something important to say. "Our band doesn't have a name."

"Becca's right, we need a name," Emmanuel agrees.

"If we're going to win this, we have to have a name other than 'student band' that Dad registered us under." Oliver makes a point. "Does anyone have ideas?"

Once again four voices break into a garbled chorus. I can't understand one word. I don't feel like I have anything to add to the conversation since I basically said I'm not going through with the plan. We won't need a name if the band pulls out of the contest.

Becca whistles. An angry nurse pulls back the curtain, pointing a finger at each of the band members in turn.

"Whoever is making that incessant whistling noise must stop immediately or leave. This is a hospital, and people are trying to get well. Oh, and it's time to test Eddie's blood sugar."

I let out a long groaning moan but stick my pointer finger out for the lancet. The band watches as the nurse squeezes a bright red drop of blood onto the test strip. Becca's face turns ashen, and I think she may faint. The results take only a few seconds.

"Hurray!" The angry nurse turns into a happy one. "You're 155!"

"Is that good?" Oliver asks.

"Considering his blood sugar was too high to register when he was first admitted, yes. I'll be back with dinner in about twenty minutes." On her way out, she shuts the door.

"Sorry about the blood thing. It's something I've got no choice to do or die." I grab the saline vile, filling the needle. "If we're going to stick together as a band, you'll have to get used to seeing me test and give myself shots, like this." Poising the needle, I inject the orange peel without hesitation.

"OOOHHH …" Becca turns away, her hand at her mouth.

"Wait a second. Does that mean you're not giving up?" Emmanuel asks.

"I guess that's what I sort of meant to say."

Rocky gets out of the chair and offers it to Becca. She looks white as a cotton ball from a plastic bag at the pharmacy. He hands her my water cup, but I don't stop him. What can a small drink of water matter? Becca drinking my water means less liquid in the bag hanging beside my bed, but I'm okay with that.

Becca clears her throat. I think she feels better because color returns to her cheeks. "Before the nurse came in, I was about to suggest a name for the band I've been thinking about for a few days." She strolls to the wall and picks up the erasable pen from the whiteboard. "A few practices back,

The RUBBER BAND

Eddie, you said the band happened because of my getting you in trouble." She pauses. "With the worst aim, you DID shoot a rubber band at me, sending you to the office where you saw the sign."

"So what?"

It's true. In all the business of putting the band together, practicing together, taking lessons, worrying about who is in charge, I hadn't thought once about a name for our band.

I can smell the dry erase marker from my bed as Becca writes something on the whiteboard. With her back to us, we can't see what she's writing. She turns around to reveal the words she wrote.

"We came together because of a rubber band. A RUBBER BAND. We are The Rubber Band!"

"Another great idea from Becca! Let's vote on it." Emmanuel's business sense doesn't waste time. "All in favor of Rubber Band as a name, raise your hand."

Four hands shoot straight up to the ceiling. My hand raises as far as it can before tugging on the IV pole.

"Congratulations! We are now, The Rubber Band." Emmanuel takes a bow.

We whoop and holler, high-five and fist-bump so loud, if the door wasn't closed, the nurse would for sure have come in and kicked them all out. Everyone seems happy until my dinner tray arrives.

"Anyone for hospital food?" I offer.

They must know about flavorless hospital food because everyone says their goodbyes and leaves in a hurry. At least, I think they leave happy. The Rubber Band will compete in the contest.

I decide I won't let die-abetes end my dreams. If anything, die-abetes will push me to make my dreams come true. I will change DIE-abetes to LIVE-abetes and never let it stop me.

CHAPTER TWENTY-ONE

NEW SKILLS, NEW NAMES

After another night of finger sticks and bleeding for the vampire, I realize I don't know what day it is. One day I fell asleep in class, and the next thing I know, I'm in a hospital bed, connected to beeping machines, and everyone is telling me I'm diabetic. I still don't know what it all means.

Dad lays snoring on the cot as I turn on the TV. The analog clock's hands are pointed to seven thirty.

Hey! I can read the clock!

The nurses explained to me when your blood sugars are high for long periods of time like mine were, your eyes absorb water, causing everything to be blurry. Things must be settling down to normal because I can see clearer. I'm not sure what normal will be for me now that I'm diabetic. At least, I don't need glasses. The world is bright and clear. I can see the leaves waving in the breeze on the trees outside my second-story window, and the cartoon channel plays my favorite show, without a blur.

Nurse Norie spends most of the morning with me, Dad, and Mom, teaching us how to manage diabetes. I find out she's what they call a "diabetes educator." She knows more about diabetes than Miss Crenshaw knows about math. I guess that makes her an expert. Someone I can trust.

We also meet with a nutritionist. That's someone who knows all about food and teaches the healthy way to eat. She

The RUBBER BAND

assures me I don't have to give up sweets but can work them into my diet by counting numbers or carbohydrates.

I'd write that word in my spelling dictionary, if I were at school. The word carbohydrates would certainly impress the entire class, especially if I can explain what it means. Will I be able to explain the word to them? All the information is getting to me. I feel overwhelmed.

My brain floods. I never think about what I eat. I just grab snacks, eating everything, especially things with lots of sugar. Now, I'll have to think about every ingredient, avoid sugar, and find substitutes for my favorite things. I'm glad my parents are learning too because I'm sure I missed a few things. On the plus side, Dad being a doctor, can explain things to me again, in the father-to-son way he does, which always makes me feel safe and secure.

Mom and Dad leave me to get some lunch. I'm sure their food will be more flavorful than mine. Although, when Nurse Norie brings in my food tray, the food looks and smells so good, I don't care how it will taste.

"Eddie, I'd like you to try testing your blood sugar. You can adjust the lancet, so it doesn't go too deep. We just need a small drop of blood to complete the test."

Holding the lancet, the pen that jabs into your finger to make you bleed, I examine its number dial. Sure enough, you can change to different depths. I put the lancet on the lowest number because I really don't want to hurt too much. Good thing you can't see the jab when the button is pressed because the lancet has a cover over the needle, but you can certainly feel it.

Time to make myself bleed. I secretly wish I could've practiced making the orange bleed.

Nurse Norie hands me the glucose monitor and supplies. I clean my pointer finger with an alcohol swab and let the finger dry. I've seen the nurses do this so many times, I can probably, literally, do the process in my sleep. Armed and ready, I put the pen cap against the side of my fingertip. My brain gives me a pep talk with thoughts of building the Lego Dad brought me. My finger waits on the firing button, I close my eyes and …

SNAP! The deed is done, and I squeeze a drop of blood onto the test strip.

"That was easy." I don't shed a tear or scream in pain.

"I'm proud of you! You did it! And 120 is a great blood sugar number." Nurse Norie gives me a cotton ball to wipe my bloody finger. "Let's get you some insulin, so you can eat lunch." Nurse Norie draws insulin into a needle then swabs a spot on my tummy for the injection. "We can take you off the IV insulin now that your numbers are in normal range."

"Nurse Norie?" I plead in a shaky voice stopping her from giving me the shot. "I want to try and give the shot myself."

A smile big as the Grand Canyon crosses her face, and she carefully hands me the syringe.

Taking a deep breath, I imagine my tummy to be the orange. I stabbed the orange, and now, I'm going to stick myself. I force my eyes to stay open for fear I'll miss the target zone. With all stages ready to go, I am the astronaut about to blast off. The countdown was on. Three, two, ONE!

Houston, the Eagle has landed!

Nurse Norie scoops me up like Mom does and squeezes me tight.

I feel like the astronaut, Neal Armstrong. Instead of being the first man to set foot on the moon, I WAS the first boy to give himself an insulin injection.

Nurse Norie leaves me to eat my lunch and watch more cartoons, but she is so happy at my accomplishment, I can hear her bragging about me to the other nurses outside at the nurses' station. One by one different nurses come in to congratulate me, but my mouth is full of food. I try to be polite and manage a garbled thanks.

I'm savoring my victory.

I can't say the same for the food.

Freedom is the light at the end of the hospital-stay tunnel, getting brighter by the minute. I'm determined to show the doctor I can manage the basics. I really want to go home, sleep in my own bed, put my new Lego together, and most of all, practice with the band.

That afternoon, with Mom and Dad at my side, I turn into a cyborg.

Just kidding.

But I really feel like I'm a cyborg because I'm connected to an insulin pump and a continuous glucose monitor. Two machines poking into my skin are going to do the job my pancreas used to before it stopped working. Some people call this the artificial pancreas, but I just call it being a cyborg. I'll be living the sci-fi fantasy life like the character on the space adventure show I love to watch.

Dr. Klekman observes as all three of us learn the ins and outs, ups and downs of insulin pump therapy. As much as I don't like this new way of life, I can't wait to get back to school and show off my "robotic" self. This little box connects the insulin to me through a tube and has so many cool sounds and buzzers, I feel like I'm wearing my own video game. I'll be pushing buttons for the rest of my life to get the insulin I need.

Wait a second.

I am a walking video game! How cool is that?

At dinner, I show everyone I can test my blood sugar, count the carbs, and press the right buttons to get the insulin I need through my new pump.

Nurse Norie takes me off the pee-collector, and for the first time since arriving, I put my feet on the floor and walk to the bathroom. I still have an IV pole connected to me just in case, but the pole rolls right alongside me. At last, life can feel normal, whatever normal will be now.

When you get released from the hospital, it's like being the grand marshal of a parade. Someone carries all your balloons, flowers, toys, and stuff while another person wheels you out in a wheelchair. They don't allow you to walk on your own. I don't care because I've never ridden in a wheelchair before, and I love having my own parade. All the nurses wish me good luck as Nurse Norie pushes me past their station. Dr. Klekman shakes my hand. I'll be seeing him next week for a follow-up appointment.

The parade continues down the elevator and out through the hospital entrance ending at our van, waiting curbside. Nurse Norie buckles me in, sets Grin N. Bearit on my lap, and wipes a tear from her cheek.

"You make me proud, Eddie. Keep up the good work and stay healthy."

The parade watchers wave as we drive away. I squeeze Grin N. Bearit with all my might hoping he can calm my anxious thoughts of the diabetic life.

The RUBBER BAND

Oliver is jealous because I get to take Friday off from school. I can't say I blame him. Five days of no homework is nice, but I'll take homework any day over being in a hospital.

Saturday morning, we decide to have band practice for the first time since last week before I got diabetes. I wonder how my fingers will do on the strings. The band has been practicing individually, and after our times with Mr. Zee, I hope we've improved.

I go out to the garage an hour before everyone arrives and strap on my guitar. With the headphones on, I strum through "Born to be Wild," feeling rusty. My fingers fall naturally on the strings without a complaint. I play through again like Mr. Zee taught me. Life floods my soul. My heart beats to the rhythm, and I am rocking out, one with my guitar and the music we make.

I'm having so much fun, I don't notice the band members sneaking in to watch my solo performance. I finish the song on my knees in a glory stance, finger pointing to the sky in victory. The four clap and whistle, calling for an encore.

"Looks like you're feeling better?" Rocky pulls drumsticks from his back jeans pocket. "Are you ready to rock 'n' roll, 'cause I know I am." He goes to his drum set and pounds the foot pedal on the bass.

"Wait, guys," Becca interrupts. "I have some business to take care of before we get started." She pulls out a box hidden behind the door. "No band is complete without a look." She takes something from the box, keeping it behind her back, and approaches me.

I set my guitar on its stand, wondering what Bossy Becca is up to now.

"Eddie, you get to be the first to see our new look." She unfolds a black T-shirt with "The Rubber Band" in giant letters encircled by an actual rubber band.

Becca places the shirt against me, flings her arms around my neck, squeezing me tight. Heat flushes my cheeks, and I want to push her away because this is a side of Becca I've never seen or felt before. But instead of pushing her away, I hug her back.

She whispers in my ear, "I'm glad you're going to be okay," lets go of my neck, and tosses each of the guys a shirt of their own. "Now, let's jam."

CHAPTER TWENTY-TWO

THE RUBBER BAND

Back at school Monday, I feel like a celebrity. Principal Haymaker explains about diabetes in the all-school assembly to the best of his knowledge, but by now, I'm an expert compared to him. All the teachers, aides, and office workers check in on me too.

Everyone wants to talk to me and ask questions. I guess this is how it feels to be popular. Miss Crenshaw has me do a question and answer time with the class. She's right about me not missing out and being able to catch up quickly. I turn in all the work I'd missed after finishing it over the weekend.

This coming Saturday is the big night. We have five more after-school practice days to perfect our sound to the best of our elementary school abilities. I know we improve every time, but to me, playing together, making music from our hearts, we already have the perfect sound.

Saturday morning, we are scheduled to rehearse for an hour on the stage of The Grande Theatre, an old opera house in the middle of the largest city in the county. Not one of us has been in an opera house before. Stepping through the back doors of the auditorium, our eyes meet the sky of a huge domed ceiling with an enormous crystal chandelier sparkling in the middle. The walls are not flat but have out-cropping

The RUBBER BAND

pillars and domes like a Greek temple. Inside the porticoes are elaborate paintings of ladies in flouncy dresses flirting with men wearing white wigs, feeding them grapes. Not my kind of art, but mesmerizing for a first-time opera goer.

"Is this the Rubber Band?" A man walking up the aisle asks us.

"That's them." Dad extends his hand. "I'm in charge of them."

"Nice to meet all of you. Now, allow me to fill you in on the details of the evening. You are number seven on the performance list. We try to keep the evening flowing, so while one act is performing up front, your equipment will be set up backstage behind the curtain. Our roadies will be quick on the change, so all you have to do is get to your instruments and wait for your introduction. The curtain will open after number six finishes, the lights will come up, and the announcer will turn things over to you."

I'm glad Dad is in charge because the band seems to be starstruck by the glamour of the place. The stage curtain is pulled back. Its thick red velvet is trimmed in gold. We cart our gear up the side steps and onto the stage.

"Set your stuff down, kids. Walk around the stage, take a deep breath, and explore your spotlight. You won't have any time tonight, and all I want you to think about when it's your turn is playing, not the size of the stage, the audience, or anything else. I want you to play like you do in the garage, without a worry. It's going to be fun." Dad's pep talk gives us a few minutes to unwind.

Becca stands at center stage, staring at the empty seats.

Emmanuel lays down his bass and examines the curtains.

Oliver checks out the old-fashioned lights bordering the edge of the stage.

I stare up into the blackness of the expanse above my head, full of wires, walkways, pullies, ropes, and other stage mechanisms.

Rocky walks around air-drumming with his sticks.

The roadies help us set up Rocky's drums and Oliver's keyboard on movable, elevated stages. The two of them look like bookends to me. Becca and Emmanuel and I will play between them.

After a quick sound check, we get the go ahead to rehearse. The place isn't like our garage at all. The acoustics raise our volume to levels we have never heard before. I feel like the notes echo off the round designs and boomerang back at us. No matter what the outcome, tonight will be one to remember forever.

After running twice through our set, we leave our instruments in the hands of the roadies and meet Mom for lunch at Joey's Pizza.

We're so excited, it's hard to eat, but we manage between us to scarf down two large pizzas, garlic bread, and pesto twists plus a gallon of soda. I drink diet, reluctantly. I guess I'll get used to it, eventually. I push the buttons on my pump to compensate for the pizza carbs my body will absorb. Not bad for a rookie.

I feel like we are out of place in our matching T-shirts, as some of the older contestants encourage us with good luck wishes. We wait in what's called the green room. It's where the next act stays until called on stage.

Emmanuel and I hold our guitars and pluck on the strings. Oliver relaxes against his chair, eyes closed, and arms folded. Becca does her voice warm-ups while Rocky taps his drumsticks on his tennis shoes. No one speaks. Dad is busy

The RUBBER BAND

taking candid photos and reminds me to test my blood sugar to make sure I'll stay upright through our set.

I've officially been a diabetic for two weeks, but there are a lot of things to remember to keep in control of my blood sugars, so I need reminding. My blood sugar is 157. A good number for the exercise I'll get playing guitar. But, just in case, I gobble down a bag of gummies for insurance.

"Rubber Band, you're on deck." A man dressed in all black and wearing headphones guides us to the side of the stage. My heart starts racing.

"Remember, band, this is just like playing in the garage. Go out there and have fun." Dad whispers his last-minute words of encouragement as we are guided by stagehands carrying low-glow flashlights to our places. Dad stays to cheer us on from backstage.

From the other side of the curtain, we hear the act before us making the audience laugh. She must be a comedian because they laugh a lot. We wait for our big moment, shaking in our shirts, staring at the back of the giant curtain.

As the laughter stops and the applause begins, the voice of the announcer sounds.

"Ladies and gentlemen, you're in for a real treat now. It's our youngest entry in the talent show. All the way from Wildwood Elementary School, let's give a warm round of applause to," his voice elevates from normal to extra-loud, "THE RUBBER BAAAANNND."

He stretches our name out on purpose as the curtain pulls back. The lights are so bright I can barely make out the audience front row and silhouettes of heads behind them. Somewhere out there are Mom, Rocky's foster parents, Emmanuel's family, and Albert. I'm sure Mr. Zee is out there too, hoping I play with all my heart. I hope I don't let him down.

Becca walks to center stage, looks around for a moment, and then does something we never expected her to do.

"How's everyone doing tonight? Are you having a good time?"

The audience roars back with applause.

"Well, get ready for a great time! Allow me to introduce you to our band."

We guys glance back and forth at each other wondering what Becca is up to. But she has the microphone, so there is no stopping her now.

"On keyboard, we have the BIG-O, Oliver Taylor!"

Oliver responds with a piano key ching-a-ring.

"On bass, we have Manny, Emmanuel Dafari!"

Emmanuel strums a ditty going along with whatever Becca is up to.

"On drums is Roadkill, Rocky Espinosa"

Rocky taps a bud-da-bump on his drum set.

Becca turns to me, her arm outstretched and finger pointing.

Oh no. My turn.

"And on lead guitar, the reason why we're here, Edison, NEEDLES Taylor."

I bow and giggle to myself. Becca has given us all nicknames.

"And I'm Rebecca Chang, but you can call me," she pauses, "the Boss."

Thunderous applause, roars, cheers, and whistles erupt from the audience.

"We are THE RUBBER BAND!"

More thunderous applause and maybe a little lightening happens too. But as the noise quiets, Becca has one more thing to say.

"Albert, this is for you. Hit it, Rocky!"

The RUBBER BAND

Roadkill counts the beat out, tapping his sticks together in the air. "One, two, one, two, three, four."

Roadkill, Manny, and me, Needles, nail the intro like we've been playing for years. The instrumental beginning earns an excited roar from the audience. I can feel Mr. Zee smiling at me. My heart and guitar are one. Glancing over at Manny, I know he feels the same way. Now it's the Boss's turn to carry us through.

"Get your motor running, head out on the highway." The raspy sound of her voice resonates through the microphone to the cheering audience on their feet. At least, I think they're on their feet. From where I can see, the front row is standing. Usually everyone follows what the front row does.

Wearing a wireless microphone, the Boss strolls across the stage standing in a new spot for each line she belts out, revving up the audience's approval. The more noise they make, the more animated Becca becomes. She steps into the part of lead singer like a pro and keeps the audience hanging on every word.

Just before the chorus, she motions to the audience to sing with her. This time, there is no doubt in my mind the audience is participating.

"BORN TO BE WILD! BORN TO BE WILD!"

I step up next to the Boss to play the bridge featuring the guitars and drum. Becca backs up as Manny joins me. Mr. Zee was right. Having a wireless is giving us more mobility, making it easier to move about and have loads of fun. It's as if our guitars are a part of our bodies as we dance across stage. We are living a rock star dream and have a screaming audience as proof.

Roadkill has a few bars of drumming stardom that take us into a repeat of the first verse and refrain. The Boss returns to center stage in true rock 'n' roll character, belting out the second half of our performance, taking us to the final chorus.

I think everyone in the auditorium is on their feet rocking and rolling with us for the last chorus because it feels like an earthquake.

"BORN TO BE WI-I-ILD, BORN TO BE WI-I-ILD!"

And in one last cymbal rattling instant stop from Roadkill, our set is over. Frozen in time for a brief second as the dust falling from the rafters settles, we take a bow as the audience's applause tells us of our success.

I understand what the word "surreal" means. This is really happening but feels like a dream.

Once things calm down, the announcer walks onto stage. "Let's hear it again for Wildwood Elementary School's Rubber Band and their version of the 1969 movie classic Easy Rider theme song 'Born to be Wild' by Steppenwolf."

Rocky and Oliver come down from their instruments' platforms, joining the three of us. We clasp hands, raise them together, then take a long bow before exiting the stage. Leaving the sound of the crowd whistling and whooping behind us, we join Dad backstage and are escorted by security guards who won't allow us to speak until we are back in the green room.

I can't hold it in any longer.

"WE WERE AWESOME!" I scream, flailing my arms in the air.

The band huddles around me, arms on each other's shoulders, jumping up and down, rejoicing together in our victory. Released from the jumping group hug, Rocky grabs me, picks me off my feet, and squeezes so hard, I feel like my head will pop off.

"We did it, NEEDLES!" He keeps jumping up and down, squeezing me. The gummy treats feel like they might make an unwanted, projectile appearance. "We did it!"

The RUBBER BAND

"It's not over yet." Becca's voice hushes our celebration. "The audience may have loved us, but it's up to the judges to decide if we win or not."

Rocky puts me down.

"She's right." Dad directs us to some folding chairs in a larger room where everyone from the contest waits for the awards. "Now we wait. But no matter what, you couldn't have done a better job. You were beyond-words-amazing, and I am so very proud of all of you."

Well, since we are number seven out of seventeen, the wait is going to be long.

CHAPTER TWENTY-THREE

Now What?

Fresh in our excitement, we can't help but talk about our performance.

"Becca, I mean, the Boss, you rocked big time!" The Big-O fist bumps Becca.

"You were great on the keyboard too, Big-O. Next time we're going to make sure you get a turn in the spotlight as well."

"Next time?" we guys say in unison.

"Of course. You don't think I put all this time and effort into a one-hit-wonder, do you?" The Boss clearly is thinking about our future.

"It's fun playing drums with you guys. I can even get used to being called Roadkill." Rocky makes us giggle.

"That reminds me." I point at Becca. "Giving us all a surprise nickname was genius!"

"Yeah, and Needles is the perfect name for you," Manny adds. "Considering your new lifestyle and all, respectfully."

"Manny, the Boss's name for you is perfect too. I'm surprised no one has thought of giving you a nickname before. Emmanuel is too much of a mouthful." Once again Rocky has us giggling.

"I know how you came up with yours, Becca …" Oops. From the look on her face, I am eating my foot right now. "I mean to say, you did a good thing taking over with your great ideas and stuff."

The RUBBER BAND

Becca leans forward in the folding chair and points her finger at each of us in turn. "I can't believe you think I don't know what you guys and the entire school call me behind my back." She stands, hands on her hips, and declares, "It's true. I admit to being bossy. I'm a control freak."

Our jaws drop, and we giggle nervously.

"If the shoe fits." Rocky surprises us all. He calls it as we all see it, only he isn't afraid to say it out loud.

"Everyone's nicknames make sense, except mine. Why did you call me the Big-O? I don't get it?" Oliver asks what I've been wondering.

"Because Ollie sounds too silly for a rock band. Now, when's our next practice?" Bossy Becca is all about business.

We certainly have fun playing music and using Becca's karaoke machine when she's not there. We agree to keep meeting but to take a break for a week, meeting the next Monday after school and finished homework.

Since the show is being recorded, we can watch the acts on a big screen TV while we wait. I don't think one of us pays attention to the TV, but it makes time go faster. We watch a ventriloquist, opera singer, Mariachi band, one-man band, a talking bird, and a contortionist, but the one that piques my interest is the final act.

An illusionist meticulously elevates a person under a sheet, then passes a large Hula-Hoop around the person to prove there are no strings attached. When he pulls the sheet away in one mighty jerk, nothing but air remains. The person is gone! A minute later that person appears at the back door and comes strolling down the aisle. The audience jumps to their feet, applauding in approval.

As the curtain closes on the illusionist, all the acts are escorted on stage to await the judges' decision. Security guards frown at anyone who dares whisper. We listen to the announcer acknowledging everyone who put the event together.

Roadkill takes out his drumsticks and plays air drums. The Boss taps one foot, hands on her hips while Manny, me, and the Big-O stare at the velvet curtain until the middle of it rolls back to audience applause.

"It's been a fun-filled entertaining night. Sun Valley has a lot to be proud of." The announcer can't finish through the audience's applause at his every sentence. I wonder if their hands get tired. They certainly must hurt by now, especially after our act.

"We only have three prizes. However, you're all winners for putting your talents out there for us to enjoy." More applause, but it's getting shorter in between the announcer's sentences.

"In third place." Out of nowhere the sound of a pounding drumroll thrums away. "Connie the contortionist." More applause as Connie steps forward, and he hands her a check and small shiny trophy with the number three on top.

"In second place, drumroll please." A collective inhale comes from the contestants waiting. The Boss crosses her fingers and ankles. Roadkill hides his drumsticks behind his back, but I know they're crossed too. Me, well, I'm not superstitious. Nothing on my person is crossed.

"The RUBBER BAAAAAND."

Wait! Did he just call our name? We exchange surprised glances, and the Boss motions for all of us to step forward to receive our prize.

"Congratulations to each of you." The announcer hands the Boss a larger than third place's trophy with a giant two on top, then shakes each of our hands in turn. Rocky's eyes bug out when he hands him the check. We take a final bow and wait to hear the first-place winner.

The RUBBER BAND

"The first-place winner of this fine trophy and one thousand dollars is." A longer drumroll holds us captive.

If first place won a thousand bucks, I wonder how much the check in Roadkill's hand is written out for.

"The Introverted Illusionist."

The first-place act had been fascinating, professionally done like Las Vegas magicians or illusionists you see on television that make elephants disappear. We didn't stand a chance against talent like that.

The curtain closes, and we gather around Roadkill. He proudly displays the check for us to see. "We won five hundred bucks! That's a lot of money."

"One hundred dollars each. What're you going to do with yours, Becca, I mean, Boss?" The Big-O corrects himself, and I wonder the same thing.

"WE are going to use ALL of it for the band's future. Afterall, this was our first paying gig, and there'll be more to come, right?" The Boss has spoken.

While we are packing our family van to leave, a woman with an up-do wearing a red sparkly dress and diamonds everywhere, calls out.

"Yoo-hoo, Rubber Band."

"May I help you with something?" Dad stops loading our instruments as we gather nearby.

"Are you the manager of the Rubber Band?" She pulls a tissue out of her matching bag and wipes sweat from her face.

"Why, yes I am. What can I do for you, Miss?"

"I'm Mayor Wendell." She clears her throat and frowns. "I'm interested in booking the Rubber Band for my fiftieth birthday bash."

Our mouths drop open so quickly our teeth nearly scrape the ground. That could have been a big dental bill.

"Here's my card. Call my assistant on Monday and arrange a meeting for negotiations. I look forward to hearing from you." Mayor Wendell strolls off to an awaiting black limousine.

"Let's celebrate!" Dad tucks the business card in his wallet, and we pile in the van.

Even though we had been there earlier, there is a surprise party waiting at Joey's Pizza. I, for one, never get tired of pizza, especially Joey's. We walk up the cascading staircase to the second floor of the Victorian-house-turned-pizza-place, opening the door into more applause and cheers of congratulations from friends and family. Everyone is waiting for us there, even Mr. Zee who had been at the back of the auditorium, relishing in our award-winning performance.

The Rubber Band sits at a table of honor with all the root beer we can drink. Dad says not to worry too much about my blood sugar numbers and getting them right because it's a celebration, and he doesn't want me to worry about getting things wrong. I'm learning you can't put diabetes in a box, expecting the same thing for everyone, every day. Things change rapidly, especially for a boy who is still a growing kid.

We all grab something to drink as Dad raises a toast.

"To the Rubber Band. May you always enjoy music wherever it takes you."

We clink plastic glasses with Joey's logo on them.

"SPEECH! SPEECH! SPEECH!" Our small crowd demands, so I guess I have to give in to pressure and say something. If I can play guitar in front of hundreds of

The RUBBER BAND

screaming people, then I can make an unplanned, impromptu speech. Here goes nothing.

"It's been a crazy couple of weeks. I never thought I'd ever be in trouble, sitting in the principal's office." Becca smiles at me. "Then I had to do community service." Rocky is smiling too. "But that led me to new friends, which led to an adventure bigger than I could have dreamed. Then I got diabetes and almost broke up the band. I'm sorry we didn't take it all the way to first place." Words stop coming out of my mouth. My eyes get watery, and it feels like I swallowed a rock. I'm feeling shaky and not sure if it's my blood sugar or emotions.

The band members come to my side. Manny, Big-O, and the Boss circle around me, squeezing me tight. I am speechless. Rocky rescues me, finishing my speech with his fourth-grade words of wisdom, far beyond his ten years.

"I think what Needles is trying to say is, we learned a lot from this experience. It brought kids together who wouldn't ever in a million years become friends. We gave it everything we had, but it doesn't end at second place." He looks directly at Becca. "With the Boss matching us up with T-shirts and Mr. Z's lessons, then the perfect name, we went above and beyond anything a kid rock 'n' roll band could do. We proved that hard work pays off." Rocky pauses, raking his hand through his hair. "The prize doesn't outweigh the success. We did this together, and now, the mayor wants us to play at her birthday. That's enough of a prize for me"

Everyone agrees and raises their glasses for another toast. But I have more to say. I hold up my hand for everyone to stop and listen before the glasses clink again.

"Unexpected friendships, given the chance, have become the most important thing to me, next to family. The band brought us together and will keep us together. It has bonded us like super glue. What I'm trying to say is …" Oh, dear. The rock is back in my throat.

Rocky rescues me.

Again.

"Never doubt the bond of the rubber band."

Meet the Author

Christy caught the writing bug in second grade after winning a prize for a five-sentence story about her dog. The teacher said she should become a writer. After fifteen years of teaching elementary school, she fulfills her childhood dream with her debut novel The Rubber Band.

At age twenty-five, she was diagnosed with type-one diabetes but refuses to let it limit her. Her diabetic alert dog, Aiden, has saved her life uncountable times. Christy plans to feature him in her future books.

Christy has written for Focus on the Family's *ClubHouse* magazine and *Guideposts* and is a freelance editor. She is a substitute teacher when she is not busy writing and lives in Northern California with her husband, close to her three grown children.

Want to know more about Christy? Connect with her on her website: www.christyhoss.com.

If you liked reading The Rubber Band, here's the first chapter of their next adventure

The Rubber Band Stretches:

Rocky's Story

CHAPTER ONE

Celebrity

"Rocky! Rocky! Rocky!" The crowd's cry grows louder and louder as I stand to take a bow. My white-toothed smile is as wide as the Mississippi River. I scratch the scraggly beard, a week's worth of growth, prickling my fingers, and hear screams of delight from girls in the front row.

Wait! When did I grow a beard?

My feet hit the floor, running to the mirror in the bathroom before my eyes are barely open enough to make sure no one is occupying it. My hand strokes the bare chin I know to be mine, and I hug the medicine cabinet mirror in relief..

"Thank God!" I'm so happy to see MY bedhead and kid face.. The scraggly beard had been part of a crazy dream. I'm glad it's not real because I'm not ready to shave every day.

Not the usual way my morning starts, but, since I'm already out of bed and in the bathroom, I might as well brush my teeth

I'm thinking about what happened last night as I squeeze the tube so hard a big glop of toothpaste drops to the sink.

Did it really happen or was it a dream?

Speaking of dreams, I never in my wildest dreams thought I'd be playing drums in a band on a ginormous stage in an actual old theater. The spotlights blazed on us like the sun—I should've worn my sunglasses. It was so bright I couldn't see

The Rubber Band Stretches

the audience. But I know they were there because Becca, "The Boss," got them out of their seats, clapping and cheering. At some point they sang along.

Oh, yeah. It happened.

Saturday was the best day ever and I know it was real because there's a second-place trophy sitting on the kitchen table. The band is going to take turns having it at our houses each week. I suggested since the whole band was Eddie's idea, he should be the one to take the trophy home, but he insisted I take it first.

Eddie has grown on me.

When we had to do community service together, and I made him fill my bag instead of his own, I figured he'd turn me in to Principal Haymaker. But he didn't. No one had ever done something nice like that for me. If it had happened at my other schools, I would have been in trouble right away. After all, who cares about a foster kid with no parents who gets moved around a lot and doesn't have time to make friends?

Eddie does.

Now I have some friends. I have the band, and I hope it lasts forever.

Sunday morning as I come down for breakfast, my foster mom, Mary, is pouring coffee for her husband, David, while he reads the paper. The golden trophy is at the center of the table.

"Well, if it isn't the famous Roadkill Rocky gracing us with his presence."

Christy Hoss

I'm not sure what David means by famous, so I just take my place quietly at the table where Mary has a plate of steaming pancakes waiting for me.

"Rocky, your picture is on the front page, and a story is in the feature section of this morning's paper." Mary set a glass of fresh-squeezed orange juice in front of me. "May I get your autograph?" She leans in and hugs my shoulders. "We're so proud of you!"

David hands me the paper. Smack dab on the front page for the entire newspaper-reading community to see is a photo of me hitting the high hat with one stick and tapping a beat on the drum with the other. The sentence underneath the picture reads, "Roadkill Rocky Espinosa rocks the house with Wildwood Elementary School's Rubber Band's version of "Born to be Wild" in Saturday night's Sun Valley Talent Show. Full story on B1"

"I'm afraid we'll have to move where no one knows us now." David takes a sip of his coffee.

"What?" I freeze while pouring syrup on my pancakes and before I know it, I have pancake soup.

"Why?" Moving is not an option I want since things are going pretty good for me right now.

"Rocky, honey, he's joking. He thinks you'll have a bunch of groupies knocking down our door, stalking you. You're cute and adorably handsome. Girls do love musicians, especially a mysterious drummer." Baby Rosie's cries for Mary save me from red-faced embarrassment as I stuff a syrup-dripping pancake into my mouth.

Mary returns carrying Rosie on her hip. Her little arms reach for me. I gladly take her as she pinches my nose with her tiny fingers, and I blow a raspberry back at her.

I love to pretend I have a baby sister. I say pretend because as a foster kid, the family you live with really isn't your own.

The Rubber Band Stretches

They're just filling in until something permanent comes along or until you turn eighteen, and the system dumps you out with no directions, and you're on your own.

It would be sweet if Rosie really was my sister. I love playing peek-a-boo with her, making her giggle those little baby giggles. Her curly blond locks and fair skin are the opposite of my black, straight hair and darker skin. If she were my sister, everyone would think I was adopted or a kid from a former marriage.

In my world, it is best not to get too attached to anyone. The Perkins' are nice people, but I am certain I will be moving along soon. I always do. It's the nature of foster care.

The house phone rings and Mary answers it.

"It's for you, Rocky." Mary takes Rosie from my arms and hands me the phone.

"Hello?"

"DUUUUUDE! You're on the front page of the newspaper, and there's a story that mentions the band to go with it!" shouts Eddie, or should I call him Needles, the stage name Becca gave him?

"Yeah, I saw it." I glance toward David who proudly holds up the front page in my direction while Mary, posing as if she wants an autograph, holds a pen in one hand and keeps curious Rosie on her hip from trying to grab the pen and stuff it in her mouth. Babies like to taste everything.

"How cool is that!"

Eddie's voice squeaks like he's over-the-top excited. I, on the other hand, don't know what to think or feel. Emotions tend to mess me up. So, I don't pay much attention to them.

"What's Becca going to think? She's the one who loves the spotlight."

"The Boss better be happy. I can't believe she'd feel any other way." Eddie's voice calmed down a decibel or two.

"She might be jealous. No, I think she WILL be jealous."

"If she is, so what? She already had her spotlight in the news. It's time someone else got attention."

Eddie has a point, but I'll gladly let Becca take the spotlight back. However, the Sunday newspaper has the greatest circulation of the week and has already been delivered. It was too late to do anything about it.

"Hey, want to come over and go for a bike ride after church this afternoon?"

I don't have a bike of my own, so Oliver loans me his. He has other things to do. Eddie and I ride to the county park where dusty trails lead up into hills of oak trees. I follow him most of the way since I've never been to this park before. We take a water break in a meadow. I lie down on the soft green grass, my hands clasped behind my head for a pillow, and stare up at the clouds.

Eddie joins me. "That cloud looks like an elephant balancing on a ball, like in the circus." Eddie points upward.

"It just looks like a cloud to me."

"Haven't you ever played the cloud game?"

"Where I used to live, we didn't have clouds, only smog."

"You had to have clouds. Clouds are everywhere. You just couldn't see them through the smoke and fog layer. Clouds are always there, creating rain, making shade, blowing with the wind to make funny shapes for kids to use their imagination and see things. Look at that one," Eddie pointed straight up to a cloud cluster. "It looks like a chicken wearing roller skates."

It takes me a minute to find the exact cloud he's talking about.

The Rubber Band Stretches

"No way. It does look like a chicken, only now it's playing hockey."

"Yeah and the next cloud over is the goal guarded by a crocodile!"

I don't know how long we stayed there, laying in the meadow grass, playing the cloud game but it was peaceful and I didn't want to leave.

Eddie takes out his glucose meter and pricks his finger, putting the drop of blood on the test strip.

"I'm not used to seeing you do that yet." Blood doesn't make me queasy. I just don't like the fact that my best friend has gotten diabetes and will be doing this for the rest of his life.

Best friend. Eddie is truly the best friend I have ever had. But, I haven't called Eddie my best friend officially, at least out loud, to his face.

"Neither am I." Eddie's number came up 135. "I'll have some gummy bears now but when we get back, let's stop at the store. Want one?" As he holds out his open bag of gummies, I grab a couple and shove them in my mouth.

On the way back to Eddie's house, we stop at the deli, and he treats me to an ice cream sandwich. Eddie gets vanilla but I like the kind with three flavors. I can't wait to eat it and start to peel off the paper while Eddie pays.

"Hey, you're the kid on the front page of today's paper." The cashier hands Eddie his change.

A knot ties in my stomach.

"Look, everyone. We have a hometown celebrity right here in my deli."

Christy Hoss

A small crowd of people gather, adding applause and cheers.

"Congratulations, Roadkill!" The cashier's words bellow to the rafters, but I ignore them.

Eddie's mile-long grin takes over his face. My face flames in embarrassed heat.

"Let's get out of here." I whisper to Eddie.

We back out toward the automatic door. Eddie, still smiling, waves and thanks the crowd as I yank his arm, pulling him outside. I jump on the bike and pedal off as fast as I can without looking back to see if Eddie's following me.

Made in the USA
Columbia, SC
10 October 2020